WINTERING WELL

WINTERING WELL A Survival Guide for the Stuck

Copyright © 2025 by Solstice & Stone

All rights reserved. No part of this book may be reproduced in any form or by any electronic or mechanical means, including information storage and retrieval systems, without permission in writing from the publisher, except by a reviewer who may quote brief passages in a review.

Published by Solstice & Stone An imprint of AGI Press Austin, Texas www.solstice-stone.com

First Edition: November 2025

Paperback ISBN 978-0-9893591-1-5

Ebook ISBN 978-0-9893591-3-9

Audiobook ISBN 978-0-9893591-2-2

Library of Congress Control Number: [to be assigned]

The author is not a licensed therapist, counselor, coach, or mental health professional. This workbook is intended for informational and educational purposes only and is not a substitute for professional mental health care. If you are experiencing a mental health crisis, please contact a qualified healthcare provider or call the Suicide Prevention Lifeline in your country.

Recipe credits and permissions appear with each recipe throughout the text.

Solstice & Stone™ For Those Who Refuse to Disappear

Created in the United States of America

10 9 8 7 6 5 4 3 2 1

For anyone who's been told
you're "too much" or "not enough"—
who thinks in spirals instead of straight lines,
who refuses to disappear,
who's most importantly brave enough to start again.
This is for you.

To my Mr.,
my Brother & my Sisters,
Mommy & Papi,
Especially to my Abby & Atlas—because of you, I am.
With eternal gratitude, always.

An Important Note

Let's be clear—I'm not a licensed therapist, counselor, coach, or mental health professional. My credentials consist primarily of lived experience, extensive reading, and an unfortunate tendency to learn things the hardest way possible. While I make excellent soup (if I say so myself), that doesn't qualify me to treat anyone else's clinical depression.

This workbook is meant to help you get unstuck, not replace professional care. Think of it like a hearty stew—it won't fix everything, but it might give you what you need to move forward.

Some of these exercises will stir up uncomfortable feelings—especially if you've been stuck for a while. If anything feels too heavy to hold on your own, please pause. If you have access to a mental health professional you trust, reach out to them.

You can always return to these exercises when you're ready, perhaps with professional guidance or a trusted friend. None of this is going anywhere.

Your wellbeing matters more than anything in this book. Honestly, your wellbeing is all that matters.

Take good care,

Chandra

P.S. If you're working with a mental health professional or have a trusted friend who gets it, consider working through this together. They might help you figure out what works—or suggest skipping certain sections altogether.

Seasons of Wisdom Series

Wintering Well | A Survival Guide for the Stuck

Spring Rising

Summering Slow

Autumn Gathering

WINTERING WELL

A SURVIVAL GUIDE FOR THE STUCK

C.I. ACHBERGER

Solstice & Stone - *For Those Who Refuse to Disappear*

CONTENTS

An Important Note — v

Quick Start: Jump Right In — 1

Welcome: Your Invitation to Winter Well — 3

Winter Rituals — 12

Your Commitment — 25

THE WINTER METHOD

W - Wisdom Gathering: Define What Matters Most — 27

    Exercise 1: First Scan—What Lights You Up? (✧)

    Exercise 2: The Real vs. Should Test (✧✧)

    Exercise 3: Body Wisdom Check (✧✧)

    Exercise 4: Shadow Awareness (✧✧✧)

    Integration: Your Values Compass (✧)

    Soup for the Season: Taking Stock—Stocks

I - Inner Inventory: Understanding Your Patterns — 61

    Exercise 1: Where Do My Values Come From? (✧✧)

    Exercise 2: What Keeps Repeating? (✧✧)

    Exercise 3: Making Peace with My Inner Jerk (✧✧✧)

    Integration: What I'm Ready to Release (✧)

    Soup for the Season: Foundations Mushroom Stew

N - Now Moment: Ground in Present Reality   95

    Exercise 1: The Truth Snapshot (✧✧)

    Exercise 2: Stories vs. Reality (✧✧)

    Exercise 3: The Anxiety/Regret Audit (✧✧✧)

    Exercise 4: Right Here Resources (✧)

    Integration: What I Know Is True Right Now (✧)

    Soup for the Season: Clarity Carrot Soup

T - Tomorrow Dreaming: Envisioning What's Possible   125

    Exercise 1: What Do You Want? (✧✧✧)

    Exercise 2: The Six-Month Snapshot (✧✧)

    Exercise 3: What If It Works? (✧)

    Integration: What I'm Taking Forward (✧)

    Soup for the Season: Tomorrow Tomato Bisque

E - Embracing Emergence: What's Unfolding   149

    Exercise 1: When Success Feels Scary (✧✧✧)

    Exercise 2: Flow vs. Friction (✧✧)

    Exercise 3: The Pivot or Persist Decision (✧✧)

    Exercise 4: Building Sustainable Momentum (✧)

    Integration: What I'm Taking Forward (✧)

    Soup for the Season: Smoked Salmon Chowda'

R - Review, Release & Rise: Integration & Moving Forward 181

    Exercise 1: The Evidence Review (✧✧)

    Exercise 2: The Release (✧✧✧)

    Exercise 3: The Rise Statement (✧✧)

    Exercise 4: The Next Season (✧✧)

    Integration: Wrapping It All Up (✧)

    Soup for the Season: Full Circle—
    Old Fashioned Beef Stew

Closing: Carrying Winter Forward	214
Acknowledgments	218
Jump to What You Need Index	219
Soup for the Season Index	226
Curiosities & Companions (Resources, kind of)	228
A Final Invitation	231
About the Author	232

Quick Start

*"One day you finally knew
what you had to do, and began..."*
—Mary Oliver, "The Journey"

Quick Start

Jump Right In

Skip the welcome pages if you need to move NOW.

What you need:
      This workbook, a pen, 15 minutes. Be messy.

Before you start any section, turn to page 25 and make a commitment to yourself.

If you're feeling lost and unclear
➻Start with **W**   **Wisdom Gathering**   27
Rediscover what actually matters to you

If patterns keep repeating
➻Start with **I**   **Inner Inventory**   61
Understand what's keeping you stuck

If you're overwhelmed by everything
➻Start with **N**   **Now Moment**   95
Ground yourself in what's actually true right now

If you're ready to dream again
➻Start with **T**   **Tomorrow Dreaming**   125
Explore possibilities without pressure

If you know what you want but keep getting stuck
➻Start with **E**   **Embracing Emergence**   149
Work with what's unfolding

If you've done the heavy lifting already or are revisiting
➻ Start with **R**   **Review, Release & Rise**   181

Quick Start

How This Works

Energy Levels—each exercise shows ✧, ✧✧, or ✧✧✧.
Match the practice to your actual energy today.
Low energy? Do ✧ exercises. That's enough.

Examples as Scaffolding. Every exercise includes examples—scaffolding to help when you're stuck, not hand-holding. Use them as templates or ignore them entirely.

No Perfect Order—the WINTER method flows
W→I→N→T→E→R, but start wherever you need.
Come back to earlier sections when ready.

Write messy. Doodle. Cross out. Ignore the lines, fill the margins. This is YOUR book.

Take Breaks: Close the book mid-exercise. Return tomorrow. Re-read what you wrote last week. Progress isn't linear.

Your First 15 Minutes:

Turn to your chosen section

Pick ONE ✧ exercise

Set a timer for 15 minutes

Start writing

That's it. You're wintering well.

The full introduction starts on the next page if you want context. Each section has detailed explanations and integration exercises—dive deeper when you're ready. Feeling overwhelmed? Close this book. It's not going anywhere.

Welcome

Your Invitation to Winter Well

Meeting You Where You Are

If you're holding this book, you're stuck. Not just a wee bit stuck, but the deep dirty kind. The type of stuck where life slams on the brakes and forces you to face everything you've been expertly avoiding.

Perhaps you're navigating a major transition, or the path you've been on suddenly doesn't feel like yours anymore. Or maybe you're just so damn tired of trying to fit into molds that were never made for you.

If conventional success formulas worked for you, you wouldn't be here. Maybe 'hustle harder' worked before, but it doesn't anymore. Rigid routines and five-year plans? Those definitely don't work for me. Maybe you're here because they don't work for you either—and this book is for you.

Now, if you're what I call 'Type Z'—welcome home. (The Hubs coined this after I asked, 'Am I a Type A?!?' and he cackled in my face.) You're the type who doesn't fit any category, who thinks in spirals instead of straight lines, who needs to do things your own way.

You're here. You've admitted something needs to change. You know the change starts with you. That's the hard part, and you've already done it.

My Path Here

This workbook comes from my own shadowy winters.

My brother's sudden illness and untimely death. The challenges and joys of caregiving, marriage, parenting. We uprooted our family to Europe for almost two years, then suddenly back to Texas. Financial crisis—everything felt like it was falling apart. An identity crisis that arrived with early menopause. The ground beneath me disappeared entirely.

I did what any self-respecting control-freak would do—tried to fix it ALL. Read every self-help book, downloaded every app, attempted every morning routine. Tried to think my way through it, then grind my way through it, to of course 'optimize' my way out of stuck. None of it worked.

Undiagnosed learning differences. ADHD. Anxiety wrestling with perfectionism. Most self-help books assume you can follow their system. I can't—and maybe you can't either. Rigid routines feel like straitjackets. Productivity hacks make me want to hide. I need something that bends instead of breaks.

I spent years stumbling around in my own darkness, trying to bridge the gap between who I thought I should be and who I actually am. Those 'shoulds' were just other people's expectations in disguise. I stayed stuck until I figured that out.

Cut to 7:00 am. Cold, deserted beach in Portugal, four miles from where I'd parked. The sky opened up. It went from slightly cloudy to torrential downpour in minutes. I had my Lieutenant Dan moment. Full-on ugly crying, completely unhinged, screaming into the Atlantic until I had no rage or blame left. Something broke open.

I wish I could tell you everything changed after that. It didn't.

Two more years of stuck. The abrupt move back to Texas. More crisis. That beach moment planted something, but it took time to grow.

This workbook didn't start as a book. It started as an act of survival.

Last year, still stuck after nearly two decades, I knew I had to do something radically different or I'd disappear entirely. Depression, impending empty-nest syndrome, all the chaos of midlife nearly convinced me I had nothing left to give or say. So I created a 100-day challenge and forced myself through it. Not because I was trying to be brave or inspirational, but because I was desperate. It worked.

When I came up for air, I looked at what I'd created. Maybe this could help someone else. So I turned it into this workbook.

I created this 100% to get myself unstuck. Every exercise, every prompt, every ritual—made for me, by me, to save myself. I'm publishing it only because people asked if they could use it too. If these prompts help someone else get unstuck, that's a bonus. Let me be clear: I'm not a coach, teacher, or preacher. I'm just someone who made something that worked, and I'm happy to share it. That's it.

I'm an accidental author who learns things the hardest way possible. If this helps you get unstuck, good. That's why I'm sharing it.

When it feels like everyone else has it figured out and you don't know where you belong... I see you. Because I am you. I created this for us. You can find your way back to yourself. You can build a way forward that fits. I wish I'd had this during my own winters. Maybe it's what you need now.

What Wintering Means (well, to me anyway)

I learned the concept of 'wintering' from Katherine May's book, *Wintering: The Power of Rest and Retreat in Difficult Times*. She describes wintering as those fallow periods when we're forced to retreat and rest—whether we want to or not.

Poets have always understood winter's depth. Sylvia Plath's *Wintering* asks whether we—like bees in their hive—will survive the cold and emerge into spring. Her question resonates so deeply because survival isn't guaranteed, but we can make our own light when we can't find it.

Wintering isn't failure. It's not depression (though it can include it). It's not giving up. Wintering is necessary stillness. Times when life forces you to stop. When you stop fighting it, wintering becomes the foundation for rebuilding.

Winters come in many forms—grief, illness, career transitions, identity shifts, relationship changes, caregiving seasons, midlife reckonings, or that bone-deep exhaustion that whispers, "I can't keep going like this."

Everything around us screams 'Power through! Give more! Hustle! Grind! Be perfect or be nothing!' Then we hit midlife and hear a new message: 'Disappear.' No wonder so many of us feel stuck.

This workbook offers a different way. A way I found to finally get unstuck. A way to reclaim your voice and purpose. To own where you are right now and use this slow season to reconnect with what truly matters, release what no longer serves you, and build a future that finally fits you.

That's what wintering well means—not escaping winter, but embracing all of you through it.

The WINTER Method

This workbook guides you through six interconnected stages. While they're designed to flow in order, start wherever you need:

W - Wisdom Gathering: Define what truly matters to you by exploring your core values and their shadows. Strip away the "shoulds" to find your actual truths.

I - Inner Inventory: Examine your past with compassion. Understand the patterns, stories, and experiences that shaped you—and make peace with your Inner Jerk.

N - Now Moment: Ground yourself in present reality. Assess where you actually are without judgment. Create an honest foundation for moving forward.

T - Tomorrow Dreaming: Imagine again. Explore what you want your life to feel like, not just look like. Dream without censoring.

E - Embrace Emergence: Take action. Translate dreams into tiny, manageable actions. Build support systems. Create momentum that honors your actual energy and capacity.

R - Review, Release & Rise: Integrate everything you've learned. Celebrate your progress. Prepare to carry your winter wisdom into all seasons of life.

Each stage includes reflective exercises and recipes for the season. Some will resonate deeply. Others you'll skip.

This is your journey—your way.

How to Use This Book

About Energy Levels

Every exercise in this workbook is marked with an energy indicator:

> ✧ **Low Energy:** Gentle, accessible practices for when you're depleted

> ✧ ✧ **Medium Energy:** Deeper work requiring moderate focus and time

> ✧ ✧ ✧ **High Energy:** Intensive exercises for when you have capacity

Match the practice to your actual energy today. Only managed ✧ exercises this week? Every single effort counts. You're wintering well.

Examples as Scaffolding

Every exercise in this book includes examples. This is intentional, not hand-holding.

If you're staring at a blank page wondering where to start—use the examples as templates. Follow their structure. Borrow their language. They're scaffolding, not suggestions.

If you know exactly what to write—ignore them completely. Either way works. The examples are there when you need them, invisible when you don't.

Your Way Is the Right Way

The WINTER method flows sequentially—each section builds on insights from the previous one. But you know what you need better than I do.

If you find yourself stuck (and we all do—it's why this book exists), there's always a way forward. Return to lighting your morning candle. Turn to a different section. Take a break and start fresh tomorrow. None of this is going anywhere.

This book is a flexible companion, not a taskmaster.

You can always circle back to earlier sections when you're ready. Progress isn't linear.

An Invitation to Adapt Everything

Write in fragments. Doodle in margins. Skip exercises that don't resonate. Modify rituals. Make the recipes your own.

Close the book mid-exercise and return tomorrow.

This is your workbook. Use it your way.

One More Thing

Before you begin any of the WINTER sections, you'll find a page where you make a commitment to yourself—not to perfection, not to completion, but to honesty and kindness.

When you're ready, turn to page 25 to make that commitment.

Until then, take a breath. Light a candle if you want. Get comfortable. Pour some tea.

Winter is here. Let's settle in together.

You can begin on the next page. Or the page after that. Or wherever you want, whenever you're ready.

What's Next

This workbook is the first of four in the Seasons of Wisdom series—the absolute fundamentals. The part about refusing to disappear and finding your way back to yourself.

The other three books dive deeper into specific challenges for different seasons. This is where you start when you're stuck.

This is the foundation.

Back to basics never felt so freeing.

Winter Ritual Basics

Simple Practices for Reflection & Renewal

Why Routines Don't Work for Everyone

Rituals versus routines. If you're anything like me, the word "routine" makes your eyeballs glaze over and you possibly just yawned reading the word. Or maybe you have visions of finding the absolute perfect morning routine that will single-handedly change your life forever and you'll n'er ever have a single struggle for the rest of your days (haha that's me conjuring my 30/40-something self)—most of all a routine that'll Get 'Er Done.

I've tried every productivity hack known to humanity—color-coded calendars, habit trackers, morning routines that would make James Clear (*Atomic Habits*) weep with pride. I started strong with the *Let Them* from Mel Robbins' latest book, but was left in a fog on the second most important part—the "Let Me." I've bought more planners than I care to admit (each one promising to finally be The One), downloaded approximately 7 gazillion apps that were supposed to change my life, and attempted more "foolproof" systems than I have coffee mugs.

What I got—a graveyard of abandoned planners, a truly impressive collection of quarter-filled journals, and enough resistance to schedules to power a small city. Turns out, I don't do well with rigid routines. The minute something becomes a "must-do," my inner rebel shows up with a megaphone and a list of literally anything else we could be doing. Then the overwhelm inevitably kicks in, annnd, STUCK...Again.

What Rituals Are

Rituals are different. They're simple—sometimes profound—ways to pause and notice what matters. I like to think of them as tiny ceremonies that help us pause, anchor ourselves, and reconnect with what truly matters. Lighting a candle. Sipping a warm drink. Small moments that help you step back from the noise.

Winter feels like the natural season for reflection. The simple acts that bring comfort and warmth. The glow of candles in the darkness, the warmth of a mug in your hands, the quiet sharing of stories—these are the moments that define the season. While many of my own winter memories are filled with gatherings and traditions, your moments will look different, and that's the point.

These practices are starting points—ways to pause, notice, and find your path through winter.

Why Rituals Work Better

The beauty of rituals is their flexibility while still feeling supported. Unlike routines that demand strict adherence (for me at least, trigger immediate defiance), rituals can shift with your energy, adapt to your mood, and still maintain their meaning. They're less about checking boxes and more about creating moments of connection—with yourself and what matters.

So if you've ever felt like a failure at maintaining routines (I see you), or if the phrase "morning routine" makes you want to hide under your blankets forever, you're in the right place. These rituals bend without breaking. They're made to work with how you actually move through the world.

Keepin' It Simple

Rituals don't need to be elaborate or time-consuming. Pausing with intention. Marking a moment of transition. These are anchors that ground your day—taking a few deep breaths before starting something new, making your morning coffee mindfully, lighting a candle as you open this book.

Core Practices

At the core of winter rituals in this book are three essential elements:

Light represents clarity and beginnings. Fire has guided us through dark seasons forever. Use light to mark new beginnings and find your way through shadows. We can use our light to mark new beginnings, create focus, and find our way through shadows. A simple practice is to light a candle, take three breaths, and begin.

Warmth brings comfort, so create physical coziness through warm drinks, soft textures, and gentle movements. Try wrapping yourself in something cozy, holding a warm drink, and simply feeling supported.

Reflection is the practice of looking inward, asking ourselves honest questions, and listening deeply. It's about taking time to understand what we need and how we feel, without judgment. Quiet moments can mirror our inner world. Take a moment to sit quietly, ask yourself an honest question, and truly listen to the answer.

Some Simple Rituals to Try

You don't need to do all of these—or any of these. They're just starting points if you need ideas.

Morning Rituals

The Sunrise Connection: Open the curtains as you wake. Welcome the day's possibilities as you create space for light.

The Gratitude Sip: Make your morning beverage, take a deep breath, and note one thing you're grateful for before your first sip.

The Three Breath Pause: Take three deep breaths before you do anything else. Connect your body to intention.

Evening rituals

The Wind-Down Tea: Pour a warm beverage, find a quiet space to reflect, and settle your mind and body.

The Evening Release: Write down one thought you want to release from the day, crumple the paper, and let it go.

The Story of My Day: Write a single line or phrase about your day. See your own story.

The goal isn't to add more tasks to your day—it's to create moments where you can pause, breathe, and reconnect with yourself. Pick what feels natural. Skip what doesn't. Make up your own.

On the following pages, you'll find specific rituals designed for each stage of the WINTER method. Use them, adapt them, or ignore them entirely.

W·I·N·T·E·R Rituals

These six rituals are designed to pair with each section of the WINTER framework. Do them before you begin each section, after you complete the work, or skip them entirely. They're invitations, not requirements.

Wisdom Gathering | Opening Light

When to do this: Before you begin the W section, or when you need to reconnect with what matters most.

What you'll need: A candle, something to write with

Action:

> Light a candle and place it where you can see it clearly
>
> Take three slow breaths, watching the flame
>
> Say out loud or whisper:
>
>> *"I'm here to remember what matters."*
>
> Sit with the flame for one minute, letting thoughts come and go
>
> When you're ready, open to the first exercise

Intention: To create space for honest exploration. To acknowledge that showing up matters. To begin with presence rather than pressure.

When you finish W, look at the flame again and say:

> *"I know what matters most now."*

Inner Inventory | Mirror Moment

When to do this: Before you begin the I section, or when you need courage to look at patterns you've been avoiding.

What you'll need: A mirror, a candle, something warm to hold (tea, coffee, or just your own hands)

Action:

>Light a candle near a mirror
>
>Look at your reflection—not to judge, just to see
>
>Hold something warm in your hands
>
>Take three breaths and say:

"I'm ready to look at what's here."

>Blow out the candle when you're ready to begin.

Intention: To practice seeing yourself with compassion before examining your patterns. To acknowledge that looking inward takes courage.

>After completing I, light the candle again
>and say to your reflection:

"Thank you for being honest."

Now Moment | Grounding Practice

When to do this: Before you begin the N section, or when you need to come back to present reality.

What you'll need: Your body, a solid surface

Action:

    Sit or stand with both feet flat on the ground

    Place your hand on something solid—a table, the floor, a wall, your own leg

    Notice temperature, texture, weight

    Name out loud five things you can see right now

    Name out loud three things you can hear right now

    Take one deep breath and say:

"*I am here. Right now. This is where I'm standing.*"

    Begin N from this grounded place

Intention: To anchor yourself in present reality before taking honest inventory. To practice being here instead of living in past regrets or future anxieties.

After you work on N, return to the solid surface you touched at the beginning. Press your hand there again and say:

"*I know where I'm standing now.*"

Tomorrow Dreaming | Visioning Flame

When to do this: Before you begin the T section, or when you feel the need for permission to imagine what's possible.

What you'll need: A candle, something to write on, a window

Action:

> Light a candle and place it near a window, or where you can see distance/space
>
> Look past the flame, toward the horizon (or just into the room beyond the candle)
>
> Ask yourself: "What do I actually want?"
>
> Don't force an answer—just hold the question while watching the flame
>
> Take three breaths and say:

"I give myself permission to want what I want."

> Write one word on paper—any word that came to you while watching the flame (or just "possibility")
>
> Keep the paper where you can see it during T

Intention: To create space for dreaming without judgment. To want things without apologizing.

When you're done with T, look at the flame again and say:

"This vision is mine and it matters. I'm moving toward it."

Emergence Embrace | Threshold Step

When to do this: Before you begin the E section, or when you're about to take action and fear is showing up.

What you'll need: A doorway or threshold, your body, courage

Action:

>Stand in a doorway—don't step through yet, just stand in the threshold
>
>Notice: one foot is in the space you're leaving, one foot is in the space you're entering
>
>Take three breaths in this in-between place
>
>Say out loud:
>**"I'm not where I was. I'm not where I'm going. I'm right here in the middle, and that's okay."**
>
>When you're ready, step fully through the doorway
>
>Turn around and look at where you were standing
>
>Say: "I'm moving forward. I can handle what comes."
>
>Begin E

Intention: To honor the discomfort of transition. To practice moving forward even when you don't have all the answers.

Alternative if standing in doorways is too awkward: Put on shoes you only wear when you're working on something important. The act of lacing them up becomes your threshold moment.

After E, notice the next threshold you cross—literal or metaphorical—and decisively say out loud:

>***"I'm in motion now."***

WINTER RITUALS

My Winter Ritual | Making Space

Release & Rise Ritual | Letting Go

When to do this: After you complete the R section, especially after Exercise 2: The Release (page 189).

What you'll need: Paper, something to write with, and one of the following: fire-safe bowl for burning, soil for burying, or just your hands for ripping

Action:
Write down everything you're releasing from Exercise 2 on a piece of paper (or use the paper from the exercise itself)

> Light a candle and place it where you can see it

> Hold the paper and read what you're releasing out loud—every word

> Say:

> > *"Thank you for what you taught me.*
> >
> > *I'm ready to let you go now."*

Choose your release method:

Burn it: Light the paper from the candle, place it in a fire-safe bowl, and watch it turn to ash. Scatter the ashes outside or bury them.

Bury it: Tear the paper into small pieces, bury them in soil (a pot, garden, or somewhere outside), and plant something new there if you want.

Rip it: Tear the paper into the smallest pieces you can, then throw them away or compost them.

Wash your hands with intention—symbolically washing away what you released

Light a new candle (or relight the same one) and say:

"**I am** [read your **Rise Statement**]"

Sit with the flame for as long as you need

Intention: To make release physical, not just intellectual. To mark the end of one cycle and the beginning of the next. To honor what was while claiming what's coming.

After releasing, write what you're claiming going forward on a new piece of paper. Put it somewhere you'll see it every day for the next 90 days.

How to Use These Rituals

Do them in order as you work through each WINTER section

Do them all at once if you've completed the work and want to create one big ceremony

Do only the ones you want and skip the rest

Adapt them completely to fit your style, space, and needs

Come back to them whenever you need to reconnect with that phase

The rituals are invitations, not requirements.
Use what serves you. Leave what doesn't.

YOUR COMMITMENT

Before you begin, make these promises to yourself:

I, _____, commit to:

_____ Meeting myself with honesty and kindness. Real growth needs both truth and tenderness.

_____ Showing up, even when it's messy.

_____ Some days I'll do the deep work. Some days I'll just light the candle. Both count.

_____ Dreaming again. Not from "should," but from possibility.

_____ Staying present when discomfort comes. Growth often happens in the dark.

_____ Taking responsibility for my choices going forward, while releasing harsh judgment about the past.

I understand that:

Progress isn't linear

My pace is my process

Every small shift matters

This investment matters

When I stumble (not if—when),

I'll return to this page and begin again.

Signed: _____   Date: _____

Wisdom Gathering

"If you don't like the road you're walking,
start paving another one."

—Dolly Parton

WISDOM GATHERING
DEFINE WHAT MATTERS MOST

Why This Matters

You can't get unstuck if you don't know what's keeping you stuck. And you can't move toward something if you don't know what it is.

This section helps you identify your core values—the 3-5 principles guiding your decisions right now, not the ones you think should guide them. These become your compass for everything that follows in WINTER.

Without knowing your values, everything that follows becomes guesswork. You can't assess if your life aligns (N section) without knowing what it should align with. You can't dream an authentic future (T section) without knowing what authenticity means to you.

Values work like a compass—always pointing, whether you're paying attention or not. When you know what yours are pointing toward, you stop wandering in circles wondering why you keep ending up lost.

What You'll Do

Scan a values list and notice what makes you lean in. Test what's real vs. "should" to separate your values from borrowed expectations. Check your body's wisdom to confirm what's true. Understand the shadows so your values don't become rigid or harmful. Name your compass—write down your 3-5 core values.

Time commitment: 1-2 hours, depending on your energy

What you'll need: Journal, pen, brutal honesty, self-compassion

A Quick Note on "Should"

Many of us carry values we think we should have—values our families drilled into us, values our culture says make us 'good people,' values that look impressive on paper but feel like wearing someone else's boots.

This is about finding what's yours—not what sounds noble, not what makes other people comfortable. Yours.

That might mean discovering you value freedom over achievement. Connection over success. Creativity over stability. Play over productivity.

There's no wrong answer here. Just yours.

There's a Wisdom Gathering Ritual (The Opening Light) in the Ritual section if you want to use it. Do it before you begin, after you finish, or skip it entirely

Exercise 1: First Scan—What Lights You Up?

Energy Level: ✧   Time: 15 minutes

Instructions:

Following is a curated list of values. Read through them quickly—don't overthink this. Your job is to notice what makes you pause, nod, or feel a small spark of recognition.

Circle or highlight 10-15 values that resonate. Not the ones you think you should pick. Not the ones that sound impressive. The ones that make something in you say "yes."

If a value you hold dear isn't on this list, add it. This is simply a starting point.

Inner Truth & Integrity	Honesty · Authenticity · Integrity · Courage · Self-respect
Freedom & Autonomy	Independence · Freedom · Flexibility · Spontaneity · Adventure
Connection & Care	Connection · Kindness · Loyalty · Community · Family · Respect
Achievement & Mastery	Achievement · Excellence · Discipline · Resolve · Ambition
Growth & Learning	Curiosity · Learning · Growth · Self-compassion · Grit · Adaptability
Creation & Expression	Creativity · Innovation · Expression · Beauty · Playfulness · Uniqueness
Purpose & Impact	Purpose · Justice · Contribution · Leadership · Service · Generosity
Balance & Well-being	Well-being · Balance · Peace · Joy · Restoration · Nature
Stability & Security	Security · Reliability · Tradition · Order · Practicality
Presence & Awareness	Mindfulness · Simplicity · Acceptance · Trust · Gratitude · Grace · Spirituality

My Chosen Values

Transfer your 10-15 circled or highlighted values here. If you thought of values not on the list, add those too.

Just write them down as they are—no editing, no overthinking, no second-guessing, yet. You're simply capturing what lit you up.

Exercise 2: The Real vs. Should Test

Energy Level: ✦✦   Time: 20 minutes

Instructions:

Now comes the honest part. For each value you circled, we're going to test whether it's really yours or a "should" in disguise.

Go through your list and ask these questions for each value. You don't need to write essays—just note your gut response.

The Questions

For each value, ask:

> Would I choose this if no one was watching? If there were no social media, no judgment, no need to prove anything—would I still care about this?

> Does this value show up in how I spend my time and energy right now? Not how I wish I spent my time. How I really do.

> When I imagine living this value fully, does my body relax or tense up? Notice: Does it feel like relief or pressure?

> Whose voice is attached to this value? Is it mine? My mom's? My culture's? My old boss's?

Sort Your Values:

> **MINE** (feels true, shows up in my life, body says yes):

>> Example: *Independence—I make my own decisions without waiting for permission. My body relaxes when I trust myself instead of looking for someone else to tell me I'm doing it wrong or right.*

MAYBE (interested but not sure why):

Example: Service—Sounds meaningful, but I can't tell if I'm drawn to it or if it's just guilt about not putting others first.

SHOULD (sounds good but feels like pressure):

Example: Achievement—Sounds impressive and important, but when I remember the absolute burnout it led to, my chest tightens. It ended up in should.

Quick Reflection:

What surprised you about what landed in "SHOULD"?

Example: Achievement landed in SHOULD and that shocked me. I always thought accomplishments mattered, but when I remembered the burnout from constantly pushing for more, I realized what I care about is finishing things well—not racking up an impressive list.

What surprised you about what landed in "MINE"?

Example: Independence was so obviously MINE it almost hurt. I've been second-guessing myself for years, but my body knows—I make better decisions when I trust myself and just move.

MINE (feels true, shows up in my life, body says yes):

MAYBE (interested but not sure why):

SHOULD (sounds good but feels like pressure):

Quick Reflection:

What surprised you about what landed in "SHOULD"?

What surprised you about what landed in "MINE"?

Exercise 3: Body Wisdom Check
Energy Level: ✧ ✧ ✧   Time: 30-45 minutes

Why This Matters:
Your body knows your truth before your mind does. It relaxes when you're aligned. It tenses when you're betraying yourself.

If your MINE list from Exercise 2 has 10+ values on it—don't panic. That means you're being honest about what resonates. This exercise helps you narrow that down to your core 3-5 by listening to what your body tells you. Not what sounds good. What feels true.

Instructions:
Take your "MINE" list from Exercise 2. For each value, do this simple body check:

Pick one value to start with.

Step 1: When You Honor This Value

Close your eyes. Imagine a specific moment when you honored this value—when you actually lived it, not just thought about it. Picture the details: where you were, what you were doing, what choice you made.

What "honoring a value" looks like:

> **Independence:** You make a big decision on your own without polling everyone first
>
> **Creativity:** You protect your morning writing time and use it instead of scrolling or doing "just one quick thing

Integrity: You keep a promise you made to yourself even when no one else would know if you broke it

Connection: You reach out to a friend when you're struggling instead of isolating

Kindness: You speak to yourself the way you'd speak to someone you love

Notice:
Where does it feel different in your body?
(chest, belly, shoulders, throat)

What's the sensation?
(open, light, warm, expansive, grounded)

What's your breathing like? (deep, easy, full)
Write it down:

Value:

When I honor this value, my body feels:

>Example: *Independence | When I honor this value, my chest opens, breathing gets easier—like when I trust my instinct to start making without endless research of what everyone else is doing first.*

Value:

When I honor this value, my body feels:

Value:

When I honor this value, my body feels:

Value:

When I honor this value, my body feels:

Value:

When I honor this value, my body feels:

Value:

When I honor this value, my body feels:

Pause here.
What are you noticing?

> Some values might show clear body signals right away. Others might feel harder to read. All of that is useful information.

Step 2: When You Ignore This Value

Now imagine a moment when you ignored or violated this value. When you went against what matters to you, let someone else's agenda override it, or played small instead of honoring what's true.

What "ignoring a value" looks like:

Independence: You second-guess a decision you've already made and start polling everyone around you for validation

Creativity: You cancel your morning creative time to handle "urgent" tasks that could actually wait, or you spend weeks researching instead of creating

Integrity: You make a promise to yourself and immediately break it, then pretend it didn't matter

Connection: You hide when you're struggling because you're trying to prove you don't need anyone

Kindness: You talk to yourself in ways you'd never tolerate from another person

Notice:
>Where does tension show up? (jaw, stomach, chest, shoulders)
>What's the sensation? (tight, heavy, constricted, anxious)
>What's your breathing like? (shallow, held, restricted)

Value: **When I ignore this value, my body feels:**
Example: Independence | When I ignore this value, my throat feels tight—like when I look for permission instead of just making the choice.

Value: **When I ignore this value, my body feels:**

Value: **When I ignore this value, my body feels:**

Value: **When I ignore this value, my body feels:**

Value: **When I ignore this value, my body feels:**

Value: **When I ignore this value, my body feels:**

Step 3: Confirmation

If there's a clear difference between Step 1 and Step 2—if your body relaxes when you honor the value and tenses when you ignore it—this value is real for you.

If both feel neutral or both feel tense, this might be a "should" pretending to be yours.

Repeat for Each Value:
Go through your "MINE" list and do this body check for each one. You'll end up with 3-5 values that pass the body test. Use the space on the following pages to record your confirmed values.

My Body Check Results:
Write down ALL the values from your MINE list as you work through the body check. It's okay—expected, even—that some values will move to different columns as you go. Different values resonate in different seasons of life. Right now, your job is to notice what your body is telling you and make a decision about your core 3-5.

YES	MAYBE	SHOULD
Body relaxed when honored, tensed when ignored	Unclear signals or mixed responses	Both felt tense, neutral, or forced

YES	MAYBE	SHOULD
Body relaxed when honored, tensed when ignored	Unclear signals or mixed responses	Both felt tense, neutral, or forced

What surprised you about this body check?

Example: *Achievement made my chest tight—I thought I valued it, but my body said nope. Grace felt so clear—I didn't even think that was "mine", until my shoulders dropped*

What did your body tell you that your mind didn't expect?

Example: *Connection landed in MAYBE. My body's signals were mixed—like I want it but I'm scared of it.*

My Confirmed Values

Write your 3-5 confirmed values below—the ones where your body gave you a clear HECK YES signals.

Exercise 4: Shadow Awareness
Energy Level: ✧ ✧ ✧   Time: 30 minutes

Why Shadow Awareness Matters Here

You probably already know about shadow work. We're not going to get all judgey about our own. This exercise is just about becoming aware that every value has a shadow side. Not because the value is bad, but because anything taken too far becomes distorted.

A value's shadow appears when we cling to it out of fear, use it to avoid something else, take it to an extreme, or weaponize it against ourselves or others.

What This Exercise Does

Helps you recognize when you're white-knuckling a value instead of living it. Notice when rigidity has taken over. See when fear is driving your values instead of love. Stop judging—yourself and others. Live your values without weaponizing them.

Example:

> **Value:** *Independence*
>
> **Light expression:** *Healthy self-reliance, making your own choices, trusting yourself*
>
> **Shadow expression:** *Isolation, inability to ask for help, pushing people away, trying to prove you don't need anyone*

The shadow isn't the opposite of the value. It's the value gone rigid, extreme, or fear-based.

Instructions:
For each of your confirmed values, explore its shadow.

Value: Example: *Independence*

When this value serves me well: (How does it help you? What does it make possible in your life?)

> Example: *Independence helps me trust myself and make my own choices without waiting for approval. It gives me freedom and confidence.*

When this value hurts me: (When does it become too much? What happens when you cling to it out of fear?)

> Example: *Independence hurts me when I refuse to ask for help even when I'm drowning. When I push people away because I'm trying to prove I don't need anyone.*

What the shadow is trying to protect: (What are you afraid would happen if you didn't hold this value so tightly?)

> Example: *The shadow is protecting me from being disappointed or let down. If I don't rely on anyone, they can't fail me and I can't fail them. But that also means I'm alone when I don't have to be.*

Body signal for the shadow: (How does your body tell you when this value has tipped into shadow?)

> Example: *My jaw clenches. My shoulders get tight. I feel defensive and brittle instead of strong.*

Common Shadow Patterns:
Here are a few examples to help you recognize shadows. Well these are some of my top ones—if they're yours too, use 'em. As with all things in this book, they're suggestions or guides not rules:

Curiosity → Becomes scattered, endless research instead of creating, starting everything at 80% and finishing nothing

Loyalty → Becomes blind allegiance, staying in harmful situations

Achievement → Becomes workaholism, self-worth tied to productivity

Independence → Becomes isolation, inability to be vulnerable

Kindness → Becomes people-pleasing, self-abandonment

Integrity → Becomes rigid righteousness, harsh judgment, using honesty as a weapon

Flexibility → Becomes lack of or blurred boundaries, being easily swayed

Honesty → Becomes brutal bluntness, lack of tact

Stuck? Google "shadow side of [your value]" or "[your value] taken too far." If what you find makes you wince, ooooffff or audibly gasp you're on the right track.

YOUR VALUES SHADOW WORK

Use these pages to explore the shadow side of each of your 3-5 core values.

Value : _____

When this value serves me well:
(How does it help you? What does it make possible in your life?)

When this value hurts me:
(When does it become too much? What happens when you cling to it out of fear?)

What the shadow is trying to protect:
(What are you afraid would happen if you didn't hold this value so tightly?)

Body signal for the shadow:
(How does your body tell you when this value has tipped into shadow?)

Value : _____
When this value serves me well:

When this value hurts me:

What the shadow is trying to protect:

Body signal for the shadow:

Value : _____
When this value serves me well:

When this value hurts me:

What the shadow is trying to protect:

Body signal for the shadow:

Value : _____
When this value serves me well:

When this value hurts me:

What the shadow is trying to protect:

Body signal for the shadow:

Value : _____
When this value serves me well:

When this value hurts me:

What the shadow is trying to protect:

Body signal for the shadow:

What shadow patterns do you notice in your values?

Example: When my Integrity shadow gets rigid—I can be harsh with myself, and the people closest to me, turning honesty into a weapon instead of a guide.

Integration: Your Values Compass
Energy Level: ✧   Time: 10 minutes

Instructions:
You've done it. Now it's time to name your compass.

These are the values that will guide everything that follows in this workbook—your compass for getting unstuck.

Write your 3-5 core values below. For each one, add one sentence about why it matters to you and one way you'll honor it this week.

Value: **Why it matters:**

              How I'll honor it this week:

Value: **Why it matters:**

              How I'll honor it this week:

Value: **Why it matters:**

How I'll honor it this week:

Value: **Why it matters:**

How I'll honor it this week:

Value: **Why it matters:**

How I'll honor it this week:

Example: **Why it matters:** *I've been making promises to*
Value: *Integrity* *myself and breaking them for years. I'm tired of being someone I can't trust. Integrity with myself is the foundation for everything else.*

How I'll honor it this week: *I'm committing to one small promise—protecting my creative time on Wednesday and Friday—and I'm keeping it.*

Closing Notes

These values are your compass for what comes next. You'll use them in I section to understand your patterns and where they came from, in N section to assess where you actually are, in T section to dream a future that's yours instead of borrowed, in E section to make choices that feel true instead of "should"-driven, and in R section to see what's working and what needs to shift.

Your values might evolve. That's life. You can always return to this section and update your compass as you grow.

For now, you have what you came here for—clarity on what matters to you.

When Energy Is Low

- ✧ Just circle values that resonate—skip the rest

- ✧✧ Do the Real vs. Should Test for your top 5

- ✧✧✧ Complete Body Wisdom Check and Shadow Awareness when you have capacity

Progress over perfection. Always.

Jump to the next chapter (page 61): I - *Inner Inventory, where you'll explore how you got here and what patterns keep showing up.*

Soup for the Season

Taking Stock—Building Your Foundation

You've just done the hard work of gathering your wisdom—identifying what matters, what you value, what you've been ignoring. All your hard work deserves to be honored.

And what better way to honor foundational work than by learning to make foundational, feel-good, soul-soothing soup from scratch?

Having a go-to stock/broth recipe in your back pocket (or freezer—it's a lot less messy there) is key to whipping up an exceptional, soul-soothing bowl of soup. The best part about it, is it's super simple and so much better than store-bought. Great for having ready after doing such important inner work of taking stock (pun intended) of your inner world.

I've always used stock and broth interchangeably, as do many of my vintage cookbooks. But in my perpetual procrastination (I mean "research") before getting this book to the publisher, I learned there IS a difference. Throughout this book, I use broth and stock interchangeably—call it whatever you want.

The difference between stock and broth: Broth uses raw bones, stock uses already-cooked bones. I prefer the latter for depth of flavor and also to use in gravies and savory sauces.

Credit where credit's due:

Dana Monsees (IG @danamonsees_cns) answers the difference between stock and broth on her website, along with her own great recipe here: https://www.realfoodwithdana.com/gut-healing-chicken-broth/

Anne Shea's *Best-Ever Soups* and Barbara Kafka's *Soup: A Way of Life* have been steady soup inspiration for my past two decades.

I have a minor (major) cookbook obsession.

Make this recipe your own—substitute, adjust, improvise.

This is your first lesson in cooking without a rigid recipe—notice what you're doing, trust your senses, adjust as you go. By the end of this book, you'll have the confidence to make soup without measuring anything.

What You'll Need:
Large stockpot (8-12 quarts)
Wooden spoon
Fine-mesh strainer or cheesecloth
Storage containers or mason jars
Patience (it smells amazing while it simmers)

Taking Stock: Stocks

THE BASE

3	tablespoons extra-virgin olive oil
1	large yellow onion
4	large garlic cloves
3	medium carrots
4	celery stalks, center leaves on
1	leek (optional)

Your Way

Choose your stock type and add these ingredients:

VEGETABLE STOCK

Mushroom stalks
A Yellow pepper, chopped
Fresh ginger, (1-inch piece, grated)
Add in Step 1 along with garlic and rest of veggies

CHICKEN STOCK

1 chicken or turkey carcass (wings, back, neck, bones)
Add to onions and oil in Step 1. Brown lightly before adding other vegetables (about 5 minutes)

FOR ALL STOCKS:

3	tablespoons champagne/cava, white wine vinegar
6	sprigs of fresh thyme, or 1 tsp dried
1	bay leaf
15	cups water (less if you have a smaller pot)
3	tablespoons miso or "Better Than Bouillon" (optional but highly recommended) **or**
2	teaspoons kosher salt *Do Not Use salt if using bouillon Freshly ground pepper to taste

Step 1 Heat the oil over medium heat until warm. Stir in onion; cook, stirring occasionally, until soft and starting to brown, about 10 minutes. Stir in garlic and rest of veggies for "the base"; cook for approximately 3-5 minutes.

Step 2 Stir in champagne to the onion/veg mixture. Using a wooden spoon, deglaze the pan, scraping up all those delicious golden brown bits into the liquid. Don't have champagne? Use water, vinegar, or extra stock—anything works for deglazing.

Step 3 Add water (warm) to the pot. Stir in the bouillon/miso or salt until it dissolves. Add remaining ingredients. Bring mixture to a slow boil, then lower the heat and simmer:

> **VEGGIE STOCK:**   Simmer for 30 minutes.
> **CHICKEN STOCK:** Bring to boil, skim off any impurities as they rise to the surface. Partly cover the stockpot and simmer for 3 hours.

Step 4 Remove the stock from the heat. Strain stock through strainer and discard vegetables (and bones).

> **VEGGIE STOCK:** Allow to cool. Stock is ready for use.
> **CHICKEN STOCK:** Leave stock to cool, then chill in the fridge for an hour. If desired, remove the layer of fat that has set on the surface.

FREEZE FRAME
Freezing your stocks is a great way to have your delicious soup stock ready to go—especially nice after a difficult or just an all-around low-energy day. Frozen stock will keep up to 3 months.

Inner Inventory

"Your vision will become clear only when you can look into your own heart. Who looks outside, dreams; who looks inside, awakes."

—Carl Jung

INNER INVENTORY|
UNDERSTANDING YOUR PATTERNS

Why This Matters

You know what matters to you now (that was W). But how did you get to where you are today? And more importantly—what patterns keep showing up that you're ready to change?

This section isn't about dwelling in the past or blaming others (or yourself). It's about looking back with clear eyes: understanding where you learned the beliefs you carry about yourself, what keeps repeating in your life (and why), when your Inner Jerk is running the show, and which old stories are ready to be retired.

Think of this as taking inventory. Not judging what you find—just seeing what's actually on the shelves so you can decide what to keep and what to donate.

What You'll Do

Connect your values to their origin stories and understand where they came from. Identify repeating patterns to see what keeps you stuck. Make peace with your Inner Jerk and work with that critical voice. Name what you're releasing and decide which old stories no longer serve you.

> **Time commitment:** 1.5-2 hours, depending on your energy
>
> **What you'll need:** Journal, pen, tissues (maybe), self-compassion (definitely)

A Quick Note

Some of what comes up here might sting. You've been running the same rerun for decades. Your Inner Jerk sounds exactly like an old boss, your ex, or even your own voice of perfectionism shaped by all of the above. Anger at past versions of yourself will probably surface.

All of that is normal and welcome here.

The point isn't to fix your past. The point is to stop letting it unconsciously run your present.

Be gentle with yourself as you explore. Take breaks when you need them. This will all still be here when you're ready.

Exercise 1: Where Do My Values Come From?

Energy Level: ✧✧ | **Time:** 30 minutes

Why This Matters

Your values didn't appear out of nowhere. They were shaped by experiences—some beautiful, some painful, all meaningful.

Understanding where your values come from helps you recognize when you're honoring them vs. abandoning them, see which life moments were actually teaching you something, and connect your past wisdom to your present choices.

Instructions:
Go back to your Values Compass from W section. Look at your 3-5 core values.

If you're starting here, take a moment to jot down your top 3-5 core values.

If it helps there's a short list of values on page 30.

For each value, you're going to trace its origin story.

Value:

The moment I learned this mattered:
Describe a specific memory when you realized this value was important. It doesn't have to be over-the-top. It just has to be true.

> Example: *I learned independence mattered in high school when I walked away from my first relationship. It was abusive, and getting out taught me that trusting myself enough to leave—even when it's terrifying—is everything.*

Who modeled it (or didn't):
Who taught you this value? Or did you learn it by watching what happens when someone doesn't have it?

> Example: *I learned this the hard way, by having someone try and take it from me. My ex tried to control everything—where I went, who I talked to, what I wore. Having to ask permission for everything showed me what happens when you give that power away. I decided I'd never do that again.*

A time I honored it:
When did you choose this value, even when it was hard?

Example: *I've walked away from businesses and relationships that weren't working—multiple times. Each time scared the hell out of me, but each time I chose to trust myself instead of waiting for someone else to tell me it was okay to leave.*

A time I betrayed it:
When did you abandon this value? What happened?

Example: *I stayed in situations where I wasn't being heard because I was afraid of going it alone. I stopped trusting myself and started waiting for permission. It cost me years.*

What this value has cost me:
Be honest. What have you sacrificed to live this value?

Example: *Connection. When I'm scared, I hide and try to figure everything out alone instead of asking for help. Independence has kept me safe, but sometimes feeling very, very alone when I didn't have to be.*

What this value has given me:
What does honoring this value make possible?

Example: *Complete ownership of my choices. The ability to pivot when something isn't working without needing anyone's permission. Work that's mine. The pride of knowing I'm building this creative life myself, on my terms.*

Repeat for each of your core values.
Take your time. These stories matter.

Value:

The moment I learned this mattered:
   Describe a specific memory when you realized this value was important. It doesn't have to be over-the-top. It just has to be true.

Who modeled it (or didn't):
   Who taught you this value? Or did you learn it by watching what happens when someone doesn't have it?

A time I honored it:
When did you choose this value, even when it was hard?

A time I betrayed it:
When did you abandon this value? What happened?

What this value has cost me:
Be honest. What have you sacrificed to live this value?

What this value has given me:
What does honoring this value make possible?

Value:

The moment I learned this mattered:
Describe a specific memory when you realized this value was important.

Who modeled it (or didn't):
Who taught you this value?

A time I honored it:
When did you choose this value, even when it was hard?

A time I betrayed it:
When did you abandon this value? What happened?

What this value has cost me:
Be honest. What have you sacrificed to live this value?

What this value has given me:
What does honoring this value make possible?

INNER INVENTORY

Value:

The moment I learned this mattered:

Who modeled it (or didn't):

A time I honored it:

A time I betrayed it:

What this value has cost me:

What this value has given me:

Value:

The moment I learned this mattered:
Describe a specific memory when you realized this value was important.

Who modeled it (or didn't):
Who taught you this value?

A time I honored it:
When did you choose this value, even when it was hard?

A time I betrayed it:
When did you abandon this value? What happened?

What this value has cost me:
Be honest. What have you sacrificed to live this value?

What this value has given me:
What does honoring this value make possible?

Value:

The moment I learned this mattered:

Who modeled it (or didn't):

A time I honored it:

A time I betrayed it:

What this value has cost me:

What this value has given me:

Quick Reflection:
Looking at your values' origin stories, what do you notice?
Are there themes? Patterns? Moments that shaped multiple values?

Example: My values were all forged in hard situations—learning things the hardest way or when I had no choice. Independence, Integrity, Grace—all of them came from fire. Defining them and seeing where they came from were my first steps out of stuck.

Exercise 2: What Keeps Repeating?

Energy Level: ✧ ✧   Time: 30 minutes

Why This Matters:
If you keep ending up in the same stuck place, it's not bad luck. It's a pattern.

If you're thinking pattern's are failures, they're not—they're information. They're how you try to resolve something that hasn't been resolved yet. Once you see the pattern clearly, you can choose something different.

Instructions:

Think about the areas of your life where you feel most stuck, frustrated, or like you're spinning your wheels.

Identify 2-3 patterns that keep showing up.

These might be:

> **Relationship patterns** (choosing unavailable people, attracting energy vampires, giving until you're empty, staying when you know it's not working, abandoning yourself and becoming whoever they need you to be)
>
> **Project patterns** (starting strong then abandoning right before completion, perfectionism that prevents finishing, taking on too much, planning endlessly without doing)
>
> **Work patterns** (not speaking up for what you need, leaving right before success, staying small to stay safe, hiding work until it's perfect, undercharging or working for free)
>
> **Self-sabotage patterns** (waiting for permission that never comes, comparison spirals, proof-seeking before taking action, over-researching, procrastination, endless tweaking instead of finishing)
>
> **Family patterns** (becoming the caretaker, always being the one who fixes things, taking responsibility for everyone's feelings, staying silent to keep peace)

Pattern 1:

What keeps happening:
Describe the pattern in one sentence.

Example: *I start creative projects with huge energy, get 80% done, then abandon them right before completion.*

Where it shows up:
List specific examples. Creative projects? Relationships? Business building? Family dynamics? Community involvement?

Example: *The book I started three years ago. The retreat I planned but never launched. The art series I stopped one painting short of finishing. The website redesign that's been 'almost done' for six ~~months~~ years.*

The earliest version I remember:
When did this pattern start? What was happening in your life?

Example: *I was 8 and working on an art project for school. It was good. I destroyed it on the way into school because I was terrified people would see it and think it was stupid.*

What this pattern is trying to protect me from:
Every pattern has a function. What is this one trying to prevent?

Example: *If I don't finish, I can't fail. If I keep things at 80%, I can still believe they could have been great. Completion means people actually see it. Completion means I have to stand behind it and say 'I made this.'*

What believing this costs me:
What do you sacrifice by running this pattern?

Example: *Finished work. The pride of completing something. Revenue from launching things. Trusting myself. Respect from people who see me start and stop everything.*

What I know is true instead:
What's the truth that this pattern is blocking?

Example: *Finished work—even imperfect finished work—is better than perfect ideas that never see daylight. Finishing is how I learn what works. My work can't help anyone if no one ever sees it.*

One small way to interrupt this pattern:
What's a tiny action you could take when you notice this pattern starting?

> Example: When I hit 80% and feel the urge to stop, I share it anyway. Done and imperfect beats perfect and invisible.

Pattern 2:

What keeps happening:

> Example: When I'm scared or overwhelmed, I hide and try to handle everything alone instead of reaching out for help or connection.

Where it shows up:

> Example: When I feel behind and go radio silent instead of asking for help. When I'm scared about money and totally isolate. When something goes wrong and I try to fix it alone instead of reaching out.

The earliest version I remember:

Example: As *far back as I could remember, maybe 3, I remember thinking if I could just figure it out myself, I wouldn't have to admit I didn't know. Asking for help felt like admitting I was weak or stupid.*

What this pattern is trying to protect me from:

Example: *Being a burden. Being rejected when I need someone. Looking weak or incapable.*

What believing this costs me:

Example: *Connection when I need it most. Help that could make things easier. Relationships that fade because I disappear. The relief of not carrying everything alone.*

What I know is true instead:

Example: Asking for help isn't weakness—it's wisdom. People who care want to show up, but they can't if I don't let them in. Isolation makes everything harder, not easier.

One small way to interrupt this pattern:

Example: When I notice myself pulling away, I text one person—just one—and tell them I'm struggling. Not asking for anything specific, just staying visible instead of hiding.

Pattern 3 (if applicable):

What keeps happening: Describe the pattern in one sentence.

Where it shows up: List specific examples. Creative projects? Relationships? Business building? Family dynamics? Community involvement?

The earliest version I remember: When did this pattern start? What was happening in your life?

What this pattern is trying to protect me from: Every pattern has a function. What is this one trying to prevent?

What believing this costs me: What do you sacrifice by running this pattern?

What I know is true instead: What's the truth that this pattern is blocking?

One small way to interrupt this pattern: What's a tiny action you could take when you notice this pattern starting?

Pattern Recognition:
Write 2-3 sentences about what you notice across all your patterns.

Look at your patterns:
    Do you notice any connections?
    Are they all trying to protect you from the same fear?
    Do they all stem from the same early belief about yourself?

> Example: *Whether it's not finishing, isolating when scared, or researching instead of creating—they all protect me from being seen, judged and maybe rejected. Seems like all my patterns are trying to keep me small and invisible.*

Exercise 3: Making Peace with My Inner Jerk
Energy Level: ✧ ✧ ✧   Time: 45 minutes

In all my years it never, not even once, dawned on me that not everyone's inner chatter is a mean task-master. Never could imagine that anyone would have the drive to get anything done without being a complete and utter jerk to yourself. Turns out, that jerk, for me anyway, stopped working somewhere in my 30s. Helping to keep me stuck for all these years. If you don't have a harsh inner critic—if you've already done the hard work of quieting your Inner Jerk—truly, I admire you for that. It's not easy. If that critical voice doesn't run your life anymore, you can skip this exercise.

Why This Matters

That voice in your head tells you you're not enough. It catastrophizes. It compares you to everyone else and finds you lacking. Pretty sure you need no introduction to your Inner Jerk. I've found that naming her helps. Mine goes by the name of Jory, and she can be meeeeaaaannn. Not today, Jory, not today.
And it's probably been running your life as long as you can remember.

This exercise isn't about silencing that voice (I've tried, failed and it appears she's the ride or die type, so she's gonna be around as long as I am). It's about recognizing it, understanding where it came from, and learning to respond with compassion instead of belief.

Part 1: Naming the Voice

Instructions:
Write down the 5 most common things your Inner Jerk says to you. Be specific. What are the actual phrases?

> My Inner Jerk's Top 5 Phrases:
>
>
>
>
>
>
>
>
>
>
> Examples:
> My Jory the Jerk says:
> You're so messy & disorganized, no wonder nothing works out. Everyone else can handle this—what's wrong with you?
> You'll never finish anything you start.
> You're too much. Too loud. Too needy. Too sensitive.
> If you really cared, you'd try harder.
> (only A LOT meaner, I'll spare y'all)

Part 2: Whose Voice Is It Really?

Instructions:
Look at those phrases. Listen to the tone. Notice the language.

For each phrase, ask: Whose voice does this actually sound like? Is it an old boss's voice, a teacher's voice, an ex's voice, a cultural message, or your own voice, shaped by all of the above?

Write 'em down:

Phrase 1: _____

Phrase 2: _____

Phrase 3: _____

Phrase 4: _____

Phrase 5: _____

What do you notice?
Is there a pattern—same person, same type of message, same era of your life? Is your Inner Jerk your internalized mean ol' teacher? Your critical ex? Your own voice of perfectionism?

This is important:
That voice isn't you. It's a recording. It's old programming. It once served a purpose (maybe keeping you safe, small, or acceptable), but it doesn't serve you now.

Part 3: What Would You Say to a Friend?

Instructions:
Imagine your closest friend came to you and said one of your Inner Jerk's phrases out loud. What would you say to them?

Pick one of your Inner Jerk's phrases and write what you'd say to a friend who believed it.

Inner Jerk phrase:

What I'd say to a friend:

Example:
Inner Jerk: *You never finish anything you start.*
To a friend: *Hey, stop. You finish things that matter to you—you're scared of this because the stakes are high. You stop when you're afraid of rejection or being judged. That means this matters, not that you're incapable. You can do hard things. You have done hard things.*

Now read what you wrote to your friend. Can you say that to yourself?
Every time your Inner Jerk pipes up, you notice it, name whose voice it is, and respond the way you would to someone you love.

This will feel uncomfortable at first. Do it anyway.

Part 4: Setting Boundaries with Yourself
One of the greatest epiphanies of my life came at 51, writing this here book. The realization? I needed to set boundaries with my own dang self. It sounds obvious now—cue the eye-roll-at-my-self—but it really did blow my mind. This idea that boundaries are not just to be set with others, they need to be set for yourself as well. Super-bonus, it's one of the few things I have control over, which makes my 198% control-freak self very, very happy.

Instructions: Your Inner Jerk doesn't get to run the show anymo'. While you can't make it disappear, you can set boundaries with yourself.

Choose 1-2 practices that feel doable:
When my Inner Jerk gets loud, I will...

> Pause and ask: "Is this my voice or someone else's?"

> Write down the thought and read it as if someone else said it to me

> Take three deep breaths and physically move my body

> Say out loud: "Thank you for trying to protect me, but I don't need this right now."

> Call a friend and say the thought out loud (it loses power when spoken)

> Journal: "What would I say to someone I love who believed this?"

> Create a mantra: "That's not true. Here's what is true:"

> (Your own practice):

My go-to boundary practice:

> Example: *I write the thought down exactly as my Inner Jerk says it, then read it back like I'm reading a text from someone else. It's wild how ridiculous it sounds when I see it on paper.*

Part 5: Rewriting the Script

Instructions: For 2-3 of your Inner Jerk's phrases, write what's true instead. (If you're feeling energized, do all 5—but start with the ones that sting most.)

Inner Jerk says: **Truth:**

> *Example:*
> *Inner Jerk: You never finish anything.*
> *Truth: I've finished hard things. This workbook. Walking away when something wasn't working. Starting over again at 50 (also at 23, and 34, 41, and...)*

Inner Jerk says: Truth:

Inner Jerk says: Truth:

Inner Jerk says: Truth:

Inner Jerk says: Truth:

Practice Plan

One thing I'll do this week when my Inner Jerk gets loud:

Example: Write it down and read it back like a good friend would say it to me.

Integration: What I'm Ready to Release
Energy Level: ✦   Time: 15 minutes

Instructions:
You've traced your values, identified your patterns, and made peace with your Inner Jerk. Now it's time to name what you're leaving behind and what you know is actually true.

Three old stories I'm done with:
  These are beliefs about yourself that used to feel true but don't serve you anymore.

  Example: I'm only valuable when I'm productive. I'm supposed to handle everything alone. I'm a failure if it's not perfect.

What's true:

Example: *I've finished hard things. I can finish this too. Hiding makes everything harder, not better. Working when the energy hits.*

One way I'll practice this week:
What's one small, specific action you can take to live these truths?

Example: *When I hit 80% on a project, I'll share it instead of abandoning it. When I notice myself hiding, I'll text one person. I'll write down one Inner Jerk thought and what's true instead.*

This week, I will:

Example: *Every morning, I'll write down one Inner Jerk thought and one **kind truth** in response.*

INTEGRATION: WHAT I'M READY TO RELEASE

This is a repeat of pages 86 & 87, which was found after redoing the page numbers for the third time. So, we're leavin' it in. Go forth and Release Mo' Stuff. I'm not renumbering this entire book, again.

Instructions: You've traced your values, identified your patterns, and made peace with your Inner Jerk. Now it's time to name what you're leaving behind and what you know is true.

Three old stories I'm done with:
These are beliefs about yourself that used to feel true but don't serve you anymore.

What's true:

One way I'll practice this week:
What's one small, specific action you can take to live these truths?

This week, I will:

Closing Notes

What you just did isn't one-and-done—honestly, nothing in this book is. Patterns don't disappear overnight. Your Inner Jerk will keep showing up (that's its job).

But now you can see it. You can name it. You can choose something different.

That's the whole point.

You're not broken. You're carrying old programming that doesn't fit anymore.

Now you decide what stays and what goes.

Take a breath. You did THE hard work here.

When Energy Is Low

- ✧ Just name your Inner Jerk's top 3 phrases and whose voice they are

- ✧✧ Do Exercise 1 (values origins) only

- ✧✧✧ Complete all exercises when you have capacity

Way to go!

Jump to the next chapter (page 95): N - Now Moment, where you'll ground in present reality and see where you stand.

Soup for the Season

Looking Inward

You've just examined some of your patterns, started to make peace with your Inner Jerk, and are now recognizing what keeps repeating in your life. That takes courage and honesty. You deserve something rich, earthy, and deeply satisfying.

This mushroom stew builds on the stock you learned to make in W. It's more complex than just stock, but still structured—much like what you've done in this section. You're building on what you know, adding layers, creating depth.

Credit where credit's due: Inspired by David Tanis's Wild Mushroom Stew (IG @david_tanis). This version uses cultivated mushrooms only—no foraging required. I do so have dreams of learning to forage without ending up on the year's Darwin Awards.

Foundations Mushroom Stew

2	lbs your favorite mushrooms (Baby Portobellos, Cremini, Button, etc.)
4	tablespoons olive oil
1	large yellow onion
4	large garlic cloves
1	tablespoon of flour
3	tablespoons champagne/cava (optional)
2-3	cups stock/broth
3	sprigs of fresh thyme, or ½ tsp dried
1	teaspoon kosher salt
1	tablespoon butter
1	cup cream (optional)
	Freshly ground pepper to taste
	Chopped fresh parsley for garnish

Step 1

Clean mushrooms and trim off tough stems. (Save stems for stock.) Slice mushrooms.

Step 2

In a wide skillet, heat 2 tablespoons olive oil over medium-high. Add onion, season with salt and pepper, and cook, stirring, until onion has softened and browned, about 10 minutes. Remove from pan and set aside.

Step 3

Add 1 more tablespoon oil and turn heat to high. Add 1½ lbs mushrooms (set aside ½ lb for last step), season lightly and stir-fry until nicely colored, about 3 minutes. Lower heat to medium. Add thyme. Sprinkle with 1 tablespoon flour, stir to incorporate and cook for 1 minute more. Stir in champagne (if using) or a splash of broth to deglaze pan, stir in reserved onions.

Step 4

Add 1 cup broth and stir until thickened, about 1 minute. Gradually add another 1 cup broth and cook for 2 minutes. Stir in cream (if using). Should have gravy-like consistency; thin with more broth if necessary. Adjust seasoning. (May be prepared to this point several hours ahead and reheated.)

Step 5

Just before serving, put butter and 1 tablespoon olive oil in a wide skillet over medium-high heat. When butter begins to brown, add reserved sliced mushrooms, season with salt and pepper, and sauté for about 2 minutes, until cooked through and beginning to brown. Add garlic and parsley, stir to coat and cook 1 minute more. Add to brown mushroom mixture and transfer to a warm serving bowl.

Make it your own, Notes...

Now Moment

*"The most fundamental harm
we can do to ourselves,
is to remain ignorant by
not having the courage to look at ourselves
honestly and gently."*
—Pema Chödrön

NOW MOMENT |
GROUND IN PRESENT REALITY

Why This Matters

You know what matters to you (W). You understand your patterns (I). Now it's time to look at where you are—right here, right now, today.

This section is about getting relentlessly present so you can stop spinning in circles and move forward.

You can't navigate from a place you refuse to acknowledge you're standing in.

So let's look at what's true. Where you stand today. What's working, what's not, and what you have to work with.

What You'll Do

Take a truth snapshot of where you are. Compare the stories you tell yourself to what's true. Identify where you're stuck in past regret or future anxiety. Name the resources you have right now—not what you wish you had.

Time commitment: 1.5-2 hours, depending on your energy

What you'll need: Journal, pen, uncomfortable honesty

NOW MOMENT

A Quick Note

Some of what you discover here might sting. You might realize you've been lying to yourself about how "fine" everything is. Or maybe that there's a gap between your values and your life choices. Perhaps you'll notice you've been living in the past or the future instead of right here, right now. This is some of the stickiest stuff about being stuck—we all end up here from time to time.

That's okay. The point isn't to feel bad about where you are. The point is to see it clearly so you can do something about it.

Be honest with yourself as you explore. Take breaks when you need them. Listen to yourself and comeback when you're ready.

Exercise 1: The Truth Snapshot

Energy Level: ✧ ✧   Time: 30 minutes

Why This Matters

You can't move forward from a place you won't admit you're standing in.

This exercise cuts through the stories, the "I'm fine," the comparisons to everyone else, and just names what's true right now across the areas of your life that matter most.

Instructions:

You're going to take a quick, honest snapshot of where you are in 6 key areas. Not where you were. Not where you want to be. Where you are, today.

For each area, answer these questions:

Current reality: What's true right now? (Be honest—include both facts and how things feel)

What's working: Name one thing that's genuinely okay or good

What's not working: Name one thing that's draining, frustrating, or stuck

The gap: What's the distance between what you value and how you're living?

Area 1: Energy & Body

Current reality:

Example: *I'm sleeping 5-6 hours a night, drinking too much coffee & sugary crap, skipping daily walks with the Mr. I used to enjoy so much. I'm feeling tired most days and not getting as much done.*

What's working:

Example: *I'm still getting up for those morning hours before everyone else—so there's that.*

What's not working:

Example: *I'm using coffee to push through instead of resting. My body is rebelling, aches, pains & inflammation are back with a vengeance.*

The gap:

Example: *Being kind to myself matters, but I'm pushing through these days. It's not sustainable.*

Area 2: Time & Attention

Current reality:

Example: I'm spending 4+ hours a day online (or what I tell myself is research), saying I don't have time to work in the darkroom. My calendar is full of everyone else's needs.

What's working:

Example: I'm protecting my morning time most days—that's a win.

What's not working:

Example: I'm giving my best creative energy to endless research and scrolling rabbit holes instead of making.

The gap:

Example: Making things matters to me, but I'm researching and scrolling instead of creating.

Area 3: Relationships & Connection

Current reality:

Example: I'm not in touch with my sisters as much as we'd all like since I walked away from our business together this summer. Too much time goes by between video chats.

What's working:

Example: When we do talk, it's great seeing them, and I always just feel so much better.

What's not working:

Example: We need to commit to weekly chats like we used to. We all want it, but not making it happen.

The gap:

Example: My sisters mean so much to me, but I'm letting too much time pass between us instead of making weekly chats happen.

Area 4: Work & Purpose
    Current reality:

    Example: *I have the retreats planned but haven't launched. I'm filling my days with tasks that keep me busy but don't move the business forward. I'm researching instead of creating.*

    What's working:

    Example: *The vision is clear—I know what I want to build.*

    What's not working:

    Example: *I'm stuck at 87% on multiple projects, afraid to finish and share anything imperfect.*

    The gap:

    Example: *Meaningful work and putting my art out there matter to me, but I'm letting 'perfect' creep in and it's keeping me small.*

Area 5: Creative Expression
    Current reality:

    Example: *I haven't been in the darkroom in years—finally set it back up this summer, a year after our return from Portugal, but I still haven't used it. This book sits at 87% done. I keep waiting for things to 'settle down' so I can get back to making, but they never do.*

What's working:

    Example: *I'm still showing up for morning creative time, even if I'm not producing.*

What's not working:

    Example: *I start things but abandon them right before completion. Nothing gets seen.*

The gap:

    Example: *Integrity. I say making art is essential to who I am, but I haven't been in the darkroom in years. I'm treating it like a hobby when the truth is—it's essential.*

Area 6: Rest & Renewal

Current reality:

Example: *I'm constantly busy but never productive. I can't remember the last time I truly rested without feeling guilty. When I do stop, I just scroll in bed.*

What's working:

Example: *I'm aware that this isn't sustainable—that's a start.*

What's not working:

Example: *I confuse scrolling with resting. It's not restorative.*

The gap:

Example: *Rest matters (as hard as that is to admit), but I'm running myself into the ground and calling it necessary hustle.*

NOW MOMENT

Quick Reflection:

Looking at your snapshots, what do you notice?

Example: *The same pattern shows up everywhere—I guard my mornings, then give the rest of my day to everyone and everything else. No wonder I'm exhausted.*

Which area has the biggest gap between your values and your reality?

Example: *Creative Expression. I tell myself it's the foundation of who I am, but I haven't been in the darkroom in years. I'm treating my art like a hobby instead of what it is—essential.*

What patterns show up across multiple areas?

Example: *Hiding. When things get hard, I pull away—from the Hubs, from the kids, from friends, from my creative work. I research and scroll instead of doing the thing. Same pattern, different mask.*

Exercise 2: Stories vs. Reality

Energy Level: ✧ ✧ | Time: 20 minutes

Why This Matters

You're probably telling yourself some version of "I'm fine" or "This is just how it is" or "Everyone else manages, why can't I?"

These are the types of everyday stories that will keep you stuck.

This exercise forces you to name the difference between the narrative you're running and what's true.

Instructions:
Create two columns on a page: "What I Tell Myself" and "What's True"

You're going to fill in at least 5 pairs. Be brutally honest here—no one's grading this.

What I Tell Myself	What's True
Example: I'm not ready yet. I need to learn more before I can start.	I've been 'getting ready' for three years. I know enough to start. I'm using research as procrastination because starting means people will see my work. That terrifies me.

NOW MOMENT

What I Tell Myself   **What's True**

Example: There's never been a 'right time'
I need to wait for the right time. *in my life. I'm waiting for perfect*
Things are too chaotic right now.   *conditions that don't exist. The*
                                      chaos is my normal—if I wait for
                                      calm, I'll never start.

What I Tell Myself   **What's True**

Example: *I'm using 'perfect' as an excuse to*
I'll launch the retreat when every- *stay safe. I'm terrified no one will*
thing is perfect. The website, the *sign up—or that they will and it'll*
branding, the timing—it all needs   *take off faster than I can handle and*
to be right.   *I'll lose control. But I'll never know*
                                      unless I put it out there unless I put
                                      it out there.

What I Tell Myself

What's True

Example:
I'm just testing the market. Seeing if there's interest before I fully commit.

I'm protecting myself from rejection by not fully committing. If I say it's 'just a test,' then it doesn't count if no one responds. But that also means I'm not really putting myself out there—and I'll never know what's possible.

What I Tell Myself

What's True

Example:
Everyone else can handle this. What's wrong with me?

I'm 51 and starting over while everyone else my age seems to have their shtuff together. I wonder if anyone will take me seriously as an emerging artist at this point.

NOW MOMENT

What I Tell Myself　　　　　　**What's True**

Example:　　　　　　　　　　　　*I need to provide for my family,*
I should be grateful for what I have.　*but I'm terrified of succeeding and*
　　　　　　　　　　　　　　　　　then failing—so I'm staying stuck
　　　　　　　　　　　　　　　　　by not trying.

Truth Recognition: Look at your "What's True" column.

What's the hardest truth to admit?

Example: *That I'm using perfectionism as protection. If I never finish and share anything, I never have to face rejection or criticism. But I also never get to build what I want.*

What truth do you need to stop ignoring?

Example: *That I have the time—I'm just afraid to use it on what matters. Four hours of research could be four hours making art but that would mean facing whether I'm any good.*

Exercise 3: The Anxiety/Regret Audit

Energy Level: ✧ ✧ ✧   Time: 45 minutes

Why This Matters

If you're constantly replaying the past or catastrophizing about the future, you're not here. You're not present. And you can't move forward from a place you're not standing in.

This exercise helps you identify where you're NOT present so you can start practicing being here, now.

Part 1: Where Are You Living?
Instructions:
Be honest about where your mental energy goes.

> **Past Replay**
> What past events, conversations, or decisions do you keep replaying?
> **What I keep replaying:**
>
>
>
>
>
>
> Examples: *I keep thinking about the path I didn't take and wondering if I made the right choice. I replay arguments and mistakes from decades ago. I obsess over walking away from a successful business recently and if I could've just pushed through.*

Future Catastrophizing
What future scenarios do you worry about that haven't happened (and might never happen)?
What I'm anxious about:

> Examples: *What if I never finish and put my art or retreats out there? What if my kids struggle because of my choices? What if I'm too old/too late/not good enough?*

Part 2: The Cost of Not Being Here
Instructions:
For each past replay or future worry, answer both questions below.

What does dwelling on this cost me?

Past replay costs me:

> Example: *Replaying that argument costs me peace. It keeps me stuck in old patterns and prevents me from enjoying our relationship now.*

Future worry costs me:

> Example: *Worrying about whether I'm too late to build this business costs me the energy I need to build it. I'm so busy catastrophizing that I'm not taking action.*

What am I avoiding by staying there?

What I'm avoiding by replaying the past:

Example: *If I stop replaying that argument, I have to forgive myself for how I handled it. That means letting go of being right.*

What I'm avoiding by worrying about the future:

Example: *If I stop worrying about the future, I have to deal with my dissatisfaction in the present. That's scarier.*

Part 3: Bringing Yourself Back
Instructions:
When you notice yourself leaving the present moment, you need a practice to bring yourself back.

Choose 1-2 practices that feel doable:

5-4-3-2-1 grounding (5 things you see, 4 you hear, 3 you touch, 2 you smell, 1 you taste)
Three deep breaths while saying "I am here now"
Put your hand on a solid surface and notice its temperature, texture, weight
Ask yourself: "What's happening right this second?" (Not what might happen, what IS happening)
Set a phone reminder every 2 hours: "Where are you right now?"
Move your body—stand up, stretch, walk—to interrupt the mental loop
(Your own practice):

My go-to practice for returning to now:

Example: *When I catch myself spiraling about the future, take three breaths, and ask: 'What's true right this second?' Usually the answer is: I'm safe, I'm okay, nothing is on fire right now.*

One thing I'll do this week when I notice I'm not present:

Example: *Every time I notice I'm replaying that old argument, I'll stop, take three breaths, and name three things I can see right now.*

Exercise 4: Right Here Resources

Energy Level: ✧   Time: 15 minutes

Why This Matters

When you're stuck, it's easy to focus on what you don't have—enough time, enough energy, enough money, enough clarity, enough support.

You can't move forward from "not enough." You can only move forward from what you have.

This exercise forces you to name what's available to you right now—not what you wish you had, not what you'll have someday, but what you can access today.

Instructions:
Answer these questions quickly. Don't overthink. Just name what's true.

Resources I have
   What I have right now:

   Example: *An hour before everyone else wakes up. A friend who gets me. Skills I've built over the years that I could use differently. The Hubs would support me if I asked. $100 I could invest in myself.*

Support that's available if I ask
Who/what is available:

Examples: *The Hubs can handle dinner a few nights a week for the family. A friend said to call anytime. There's a free community class at the library I could join.*

Skills I'm not using
What I know how to do:

Examples: *I'm good at organizing events—I planned creative retreats in my head and momcations IRL for years. I can write, but I haven't finished and shared anything. I'm a natural leader, but I've been hiding.*

Time I'm not using well
What time do you have that you're spending on things that don't serve you?

Example: *Hours a day on distracted scrolling and research rabbit holes. Mornings I protect but then give away to everyone else's needs. Evening time after everyone's settled that I spend researching instead of creating.*

What's already working

What's functioning in your life right now that you take for granted?

> Example: *I still get up early most days. I protect my morning time even if I don't always use it well. The Hubs supports me without question. I haven't quit even when I wanted to.*

Small wins I'm ignoring

What have you already done that proves you can do hard things?

> Example: *I handled all the logistics for the Portugal move and the move back. I've restarted so many times and survived. I got up this morning even though I didn't want to. I opened this workbook.*

One thing I could do with what I have:

> Example: *With 30 minutes in the morning and the notebook I already own, I could start writing again. I don't need anything else to begin.*

Integration: What I Know Is True Right Now

Energy Level: ✧   Time: 15 minutes

Instructions:
You've taken an honest look at where you are. Now it's time to name what you're taking forward.

Three truths about where I am:
What do you know for sure about your current reality?

Examples: I'm more tired than I've been admitting. The gap between my values and my life is bigger than I thought. I have more resources than I've been acknowledging.

Where I've been living (and where I'm choosing to be now):
Have you been replaying the past or catastrophizing about the future? Where are you choosing to be?

Example: I've been replaying having shut down another business and worrying about whether it's too late to start over. But right now, in this moment, I'm here with what I have. That's where I'm choosing to be. Time to get back to "Relentlessly Present.", (lil' something I used to repeat to myself).

What I have right now that I'm ready to use
What resource, skill, or support are you committing to use?

> Example: 30 morning minutes. My darkroom that's finally set up. The Hubs and family who'd support me if I asked. Proof that I've restarted before and survived

One thing I'm ready to stop pretending about:

What story are you done telling yourself?

> Example: I'm done pretending I'm fine with how things are. It's not fine. Period.

One small step I can take from here:

What's one tiny action you can take from where you are?

> Example: I can start using a dedicated 30 morning minutes for myself. Annnd Done.

Closing Notes

Being present isn't easy. Some part of you wants to live in the past (where at least you know what happened) or the future (where you can control the story). But you can't change the past, and you can't live in the future.

You can only be here. Now.

"Here" might not be where you want to be, but it's where you are. And that's your starting point.

You can't navigate from a fantasy, no matter how hard you try. You can only navigate from the truth.

So now you know where you're standing.

Take a breath. You did hard work here.

When Energy Is Low
- ✧ Just do Exercise 4 (Right Here Resources) to ground yourself in what you have
- ✧ ✧ Do Exercises 1 & 2 (Truth Snapshot and Stories vs. Reality)
- ✧ ✧ ✧ Complete all exercises when you have capacity

Start from where you are.

Jump to the next chapter (page 125): T - Tomorrow Dreaming, where you'll envision what's possible from here.

Soup for the Season

Present Reality—Nourishing Clarity

You've gotten brutally honest about where you are. You've looked at the gap between your values and your reality. You've named your resources. Now you need something to ground you in all that clarity.

This carrot soup is bright and straightforward—just like the truth you just told yourself. The basic technique is here, but you can adapt it. Want more ginger? Add it. Prefer it spicy? Go for it. Trust yourself to make adjustments based on what feels right.

Credit where credit's due: This recipe is inspired by Melissa Clark's (IG @clarkbar) Lemony Carrot and ~~Cauliflower~~ Soup: https://cooking.nytimes.com/recipes/1015360-lemony-carrot-and-cauliflower-soup

Clarity Carrot Soup

3	tablespoons extra-virgin olive oil, more for serving
1	large yellow onion, peeled and diced (2 cups)
4	large garlic cloves, chopped
1	tablespoon fresh ginger, grated
10	medium carrots (2 lbs), peeled cut into ½-inch pieces
1½	teaspoons kosher salt, more as desired
3	tablespoons champagne/wine OR cider vinegar, to deglaze pan
2	tablespoons miso or "Better Than Bouillon" (Chicken or Veggie)
4	cups water or broth
1	can coconut milk
½	teaspoon lemon zest
2	tablespoons lemon juice, more to taste
	Coarse sea salt, for serving
	Cilantro leaves (if it doesn't taste like soap to you) or flat-leaf parsley, for serving

Step 1
Heat the oil over medium heat until warm. Stir in onion; cook, stirring occasionally, until soft and lightly colored, 7 to 10 minutes. Stir in garlic and cook for 1 minute. Trust your eyes and nose here—when the onions are clear and fragrant, you're ready for the next step.

Step 2
Stir in champagne/wine or cider vinegar to deglaze the pan. Using a wooden spoon, bring up all those delicious golden brown bits into the liquid.

Step 3

Add carrots, ginger, salt and 4 cups water to the pot. Stir in the bouillon/miso until it dissolves. Bring mixture to a simmer and cook, uncovered, 5 minutes. Cook over medium-low heat until the vegetables are very tender, about 10-15 minutes. Test a carrot piece with a fork—if it slides through easily, you're done. Trust your fork over the timer.

Step 4

Stir in can of coconut milk. Remove the soup from the heat. Using an immersion blender, puree the soup until smooth. (Alternatively, you can let soup cool slightly then puree it in batches in a food processor or blender.) If necessary, return the pureed soup to the heat to warm through. Stir in the lemon zest and juice just before serving.

Taste it. Need more zinnngg? Add more lemon. Want it richer? Drizzle more oil. Season with sea salt and fresh herbs to your taste.

Make it your own...

Want it spicier? Add red pepper flakes with the garlic or a pinch of cayenne at the end.

Prefer it sweeter? Add a teaspoon of maple syrup or honey before blending.

Don't have coconut milk? Use cream, whole milk, or skip it entirely for a lighter soup.

No fresh ginger? Use ½ teaspoon ground ginger (or leave it out).

The amounts here are guides, not rules. Trust your taste buds.

Tomorrow Dreaming

"When I dare to be powerful, to use my strength in the service of my vision, then it becomes less and less important whether I am afraid."
—Audre Lorde

TOMORROW DREAMING |
ENVISIONING WHAT'S POSSIBLE

Why This Matters

You've done the hard work. You know what matters to you (W). You understand your patterns (I). You've gotten brutally honest about where you are right now (N).

Now it's time to look forward—to use the momentum you've been building and start designing a life that's yours.

First, you need to invite yourself to imagine the possibilities. Dreams that have been dormant for years. New ones you've dismissed as too impractical. Let's dust them off.

This is about giving those dreams wings and giving full attention to the one person who deserves it most—you. This is about looking at where you are and re-imagining what's possible from here.

What You'll Do

Strip away the "should" dreams and find what you want. Create a realistic six-month vision from where you're standing. Scale your desires down to the smallest version that still matters. Ask "what if it works?" instead of catastrophizing about failure.

Time commitment: 2-2.5 hours, depending on your energy

What you'll need: Journal, pen, willingness to want things without apologizing for them

A Quick Note

This section is an invitation to reconnect with what you want your life to look like. To imagine possibilities you may have set aside years ago, or dreams you've never allowed yourself to speak out loud.

You can start again. You can choose differently. You can build a life that feels like yours.

The dreams you uncover here might surprise you. They might be quieter than you expected, or bigger, or completely different from what you thought you should want.

This is about rediscovering your purpose and pursuing it—six months from now, with the resources you identified in N, from the truth you just admitted to yourself.

You can want what you want. You choose what happens next.

So let's figure out where you're going.

Exercise 1: What Do You Want

Energy Level: ✧ ✧ ✧   Time: 45 minutes

Why This Matters

You've been living with what you think you should want for so long that you might have lost touch with what you truly want.

There's the version of your dreams that sounds good when you say it out loud—the one that would look impressive, the one that fits the narrative you've been telling yourself about who you're supposed to be. Or maybe you've stopped dreaming altogether because you don't believe you deserve to want things.

Annnnnd then there's the real version. The one that lives underneath all that noise. The one that's been waiting for you to pay attention.

This exercise helps you strip away the performance and reconnect with the desire underneath. Honestly you can't pursue what matters to you if you're chasing someone else's definition of success.

Instructions:
You're going to work through three layers for each area: the Surface Dream (what you think you should want), the Real Dream (what you want), and the Core Desire (why you want it).

Be honest with yourself. These answers are for you. They're the foundation for building a life that feels aligned with who you are.

Area 1: Work & Purpose

The Surface Dream
What's the impressive-sounding version of what you want?

Example: *I want a retrospective at a major museum, work in permanent collections, critical acclaim, sold-out retreats with waiting lists. I want to be known as an artist who proved you can start over in midlife and make it*

The Real Dream
Strip away what looks good. What do you want?

Example: *I want to make a living doing creative work I love. I want to sell art that matters to me without needing gallery representation. I want to create experiences that bring people together. I want to support my family while doing work that's mine.*

The Core Desire:
Why do you want this? What would it give you?

Example: *Proof that I can build something meaningful in my second half. The ability to support my family while doing work that brings me alive. Freedom to work in intense bursts when inspiration hits, not according to someone else's schedule.*

Area 2: Relationships & Connection

The Surface Dream
What's the Hallmark-movie version?

Example: *I want to be able to fly my friends and family in for visits, treat them to spa weekends and adventures, create regular reunions where we can all be together despite the distance.*

The Real Dream
What would feed you?

Example: *I want to see my friends and family more than once or twice a year. I want to create space for the people who matter instead of letting distance keep us apart. I want connection that doesn't require elaborate planning—just the ability to say 'come visit' and make it happen.*

The Core Desire:
What are you really looking for?

Example: *To stay close to the people who know me, despite the miles between us and my tendency to isolate. To not let distance or my own patterns erode relationships that matter. To have the resources to prioritize connection and relationships.*

Area 3: Creative Expression

The Surface Dream
What's the Instagram-worthy version?

Example: *I want gallery shows, art features in magazines, a beautiful studio space, consistent art sales, world-wide recognition as a serious artist.*

The Real Dream
What would you do if no one was watching?

Example: *I want to spend time in the darkroom, writing and painting without worrying if they'll sell. I want to write because it helps me think. I want to paint when the urge hits without needing it to become anything more. I want to create for the sake of creating*

The Core Desire:
What would this give you?

Example: *A sense of fulfillment and purpose. Proof that I'm more than the roles I play. A way to process and express what's happening in my life. Connection to the part of me that existed before.*

Area 4: How You Spend Your Days

The Surface Dream
What does the "intentional life" look like?

Example: : I want to finish a project every month like clockwork, work with complete focus, exercise daily, eat perfectly, show up for my family, maintain all my friendships, and never get overwhelmed or burn out.

The Real Dream
What would feel good?

Example: I want mornings before everyone else wakes up. I want to reach out instead of pulling away. I want one day a week that's mine. I want to work my way along with rest when I need it and not feel guilty about it.

The Core Desire:
What are you really after?

Example: Room to breathe. Time that's actually mine. Staying close to people instead of disappearing. Rest without the guilt story that follows it.

Truth Recognition

Look at your "Real Dream" and "Core Desire" answers.

What do you notice?

How do your real dreams compare to what you thought you wanted?

What surprised you?

Where did you discover the surface dream was about someone else's expectations?

What do you want?

If you could organize your life around one core desire for the next six months, what would it be?

Example: *I noticed that most of my surface dreams were about achievement and looking like I have it all together. What I want is simple—To make art, support my family, work my way, stay connected. If I organized around one core desire for six months, it would be freedom.* **The smallest version:** *guard three mornings a week for creative time. To choose one 87% done project and focus on that until it's finished and shared.*

Exercise 2: The Six-Month Snapshot

Energy Level: ✧✧   Time: 30 minutes

Why This Matters

Most future visioning asks you to imagine your life years from now. That's never worked for me. My swirly mind struggles to hold anything that far away as a real possibility.

Six months is different. Six months is close enough to touch, to make it real. Close enough that you can see how you'd get from here to there. Close enough to act on.

This exercise asks you to imagine where you could realistically be in six months if you made choices aligned with what you want. You're creating a bridge between where you are now and where you want to go.

Instructions: It's six months from now. You're sitting where you are right now, and things have shifted.

You made choices aligned with what matters to you. You acted on what you learned about yourself.
Answer these questions in present tense, as if it's already true.

It's 6 months from now. What's different?
    What's different in my life:

    Example: *This book is published—I proved I could finish something. I'm working in the darkroom regularly again. I've sold several pieces of art. I'm providing for my family and helping people. I'm building my life on my terms.*

What changed to make this possible?
What I did differently:

Example: *I finished the book even though it's far from perfect. I finished and shared my art instead of keeping it hidden. I made my morning creative time a non-negotiable. I asked for help when I needed it instead of hiding.*

What am I doing regularly that I'm not doing now?
New habits or practices:

Example: *I'm in the darkroom at least twice a week. I'm finishing and sharing work instead of perfecting it endlessly. I'm reaching out to friends instead of hiding when things get hard. I'm treating my creative time as real work, not a hobby I'll get to eventually.*

What did I stop doing?
What I let go of:

Example: *I stopped researching and started creating. I stopped waiting for the perfect time. I stopped hiding my work and started showing it to people. I stopped apologizing for wanting to be an artist.*

How do I feel different?
How I feel:

Example: *More grounded and proud of myself. Like I'm creating instead of just thinking about it. I still have hard days, but I have evidence now that I can finish what I start and share it with others. That there's value in my art and ideas. I feel like an artist, not someone who hopes to be one someday.*

What surprised me about this six months?
What surprised me:

Example: *How much I was standing in my own way, again. How small the first steps needed to be. How good it feels to keep a promise to myself. That people are moved by what I'm creating and genuinely interested in my work.*

Reality Check:
Look at what you wrote.

Is this achievable from where you are right now?

With what you have and what you know?

What would need to be true for this to happen?

What conversations, decisions, or changes would move you in this direction?

What's one thing you could do this week that would point you toward this future?

What's the first step?

Example: *Yes, this is achievable. I have morning time, resources, and skills. What needs to happen. FINISH and send the book this month, stop perfecting and start sharing, start walking with the Hubs again to get time back with him and move my body.* **This week:** *finish last edits and photograph three pieces for a friend.* **First step:** *open the book file first thing tomorrow, finish by Friday.*

Exercise 3: What If This Works?
(and What Would Make It Easy?)

Energy Level: ✧   Time: 15 minutes

Why This Matters

You've spent a lot of mental energy imagining what could go wrong. What if you fail? What if it's too hard? What if you're not ready?

Now flip it. What could go right? What if you try and it really works? What if you succeed?

I know I get in my head and usually make things waaayyy more difficult than they need to be. Yet, there's a better way. We're allowed to make things easy. Making something difficult doesn't make it more valuable. Sometimes the simplest path forward is the one that gets you there.

Instructions:
Answer following questions quickly and honestly. Imagine success. Explore what would make this easier rather than harder.

What if it works?
Pick one thing from your six-month snapshot. Imagine it happens:

Example: What if I do finish and publish the book? What if someone reads it and tells me it helped them? What if I have my first solo art show and people are moved by my work? What if the retreats sell out?

What becomes possible if it works?
Beyond the immediate thing—what opens up?

> Example: *If I prove to myself I can finish and share the book, I start believing I can finish anything. If the book helps just one person get unstuck, it was worth it. If I get one new collector, I start seeing myself as a working artist instead of someone who hopes to be one someday.*

What's the best-case scenario?
Go ahead. Imagine it—the best version.

> Example: *Best case, the book helps people who feel stuck find their purpose again. My art is collected and people value the work. I'm making a living doing creative work— proving to myself and my family that integrity means walking the walk.*

What would make this ridiculously easy?
What would remove friction and make this something you'd want to do?

> Example: *If I batched the small boring parts (export files, write descriptions) in one sitting. If I photographed three pieces of art and sent them to people who've asked to see my work. If I stopped making everything harder than it needs to be.*

What small thing could I do this week that would make it easier?
Just one thing that removes friction or adds support.
One thing I could do:

Example: *I could finish the last edits on the book. I could photograph three pieces and send them to a friend who's been asking to see my work. I could reach out to one friend instead of hiding. I could tell the Hubs I need help with something specific. Uhggg self that's more than one thing, lol.*

Quick Reflection

What shifted when you imagined success instead of failure?

What would make this easier that you've been hesitant to do? (Asking for help? Adjusting your standards? Starting smaller?)

What's one thing you could do today to make next week more doable?

Example: *When I imagined it working instead of failing, I realized how much energy I waste catastrophizing. Asking the Hubs or mom to read the book layout would make things easier. I haven't because I don't want to bother them, but both are always happy to help. One thing I could do today: finish that last chapter edit I've been avoiding and just get 'er done.*

Integration: What I'm Taking Forward

Energy Level: ✧   Time: 15 minutes

Instructions:
You've envisioned what's possible. You've scaled it to something meaningful and doable. You've imagined it working. Now name what you're taking forward.

What do I want?
  At the core, what matters most?

  Examples: I want to finish this book and help people who feel stuck. I want collectors for my art and make a living doing creative work. I want to prove to myself that it's not too late to start again—that I can do it, and do it my way. To show up for myself by living my values.

Where could I be in six months?
  What becomes possible if you make aligned choices?

  Example: I could have the book published and helping people. I could have a couple of collectors and sold-out retreats. I could be contributing financially to my family while doing work I love. I could be creating regularly and connecting with my people. I could be building this creative life on my terms—my way.

What would make this easier?
What support could you ask for? What friction could you remove?

Examples: *I could ask the Hubs to handle mornings on editing days. I could ask my mom to look at the book layout. I could give myself permission to put the book out there before it feels perfect.*

One thing I'm committing to this week:
Just one thing. One step forward.

Example: *I'm finishing the book layout this week. That's my commitment. Everything else can wait, but this gets done.*

Closing Notes

It's never too late to start again. It's never too late to choose differently. It's never too late to build a life that honors what matters to you.

The future you're imagining doesn't require you to become someone else. It requires you to reconnect with who you are and make choices aligned with that truth.

You've identified what you want. You've envisioned where you could be. You've imagined it working.

Now you know where you're headed. You have a direction. You have a next step.

Six months from now, with what you have, from where you are—this is possible.

When Energy Is Low

- ✧ Just do Exercise 3 (What If It Works?) to practice imagining success instead of catastrophizing
- ✧✧ Do Exercise 2 (Six-Month Snapshot) to envision where you could be
- ✧✧✧ Start with Exercise 1 (What Do You Want), then do the rest if you're up to it.

Dream it, then do it. That's how it works, y'all!

Jump to the next chapter (page 149): E - Embracing Emergence, where you'll figure out what to do with all this clarity—not a perfect plan, just the next right move from where you're standing.

Soup for the Season

Your Own Creation—Born from Need

You've envisioned what's possible. You've imagined it working. Now you need to eat.

This tomato bisque is my own creation, born from necessity during my "Sandwich Gen" caregiving years. I needed an easy, fast, nourishing meal that would satisfy my tenacious toddler Abby and my 101-year-old fiery grandmother-in-law at the same time.

This is what happens when you create from where you are, with what you have. You can do the same.

Credit where credit's due: This one is my own through and through. I have an impractically large cookbook collection—vintage cookbooks, handwritten recipe cards, the works. I love cooking, soups tho', are my jam. But my favorite recipes are the ones passed down through generations. This tomato bisque draws on those time-honored traditions, the kind that reach back to simpler times when you made do with what you had.

Tomorrow Tomato Bisque

3	tablespoons extra-virgin olive oil, more for serving
1	large yellow onion, peeled and diced (2 cups)
4-8	large garlic cloves, chopped
2	(28 oz) cans tomatoes (whole, diced, crushed, or puree—any style works)
2	medium carrots, chopped
2-3	celery stalks, chopped
3	tablespoons cider vinegar or dry white wine/champagne, to deglaze pan
3	tablespoons "Better Than Bouillon" (Chicken or Veggie)
4	cups water or broth
4-6	sprigs of thyme
3	bay leaves (great substitutes are olive, oak or grapevine leaves)

Handful fresh basil
½ cup heavy cream, whole milk, or coconut milk
Coarse sea salt and fresh ground pepper, for serving

Step 1

Heat the oil over medium heat until warm. Stir in onion, carrots, and celery; cook, stirring occasionally, until soft and lightly colored, 7 to 10 minutes. Stir in garlic and cook for 1 minute.

Step 2

Stir in champagne/wine or cider vinegar to deglaze the pan. Using a wooden spoon, bring up all those delicious golden brown bits into the liquid.

Step 3

Add tomatoes (if using whole, break them up with a spoon) and stir to combine. Add 4 cups water or broth to the pot. Stir in the bouillon until it dissolves. Add thyme and bay leaves. Bring mixture to a simmer and cook, uncovered, 5 minutes. Lower heat to medium-low and cook about 20 minutes.

Step 4

Remove bay leaves and woody parts of thyme sprigs. Stir in cream, whole milk, or coconut milk. Remove the soup from the heat. Using an immersion blender, puree the soup until smooth. (Alternatively, you can let soup cool slightly then puree it in batches in a food processor or blender.) Stir in shredded fresh basil leaves (set aside about ½ for garnish). Return the pureed soup to the heat to warm through. Drizzle with oil, sea salt, fresh ground pepper, and sprinkle with some shredded basil leaves.

Make it your own, Notes...

Embracing Emergence

*"If the time is not ripe,
we have to ripen the time."*
—Dorothy Height

EMBRACING EMERGENCE |
WORK WITH WHAT'S UNFOLDING

Why This Matters

You've done the hard work. You know what matters to you (W). You understand your patterns (I). You've gotten brutally honest about where you are right now (N). You've envisioned what's possible and maybe even taken some steps toward it (T).

Now, things are moving. Some might say unstuck.

You took that first step and it felt good. Or momentum is building and you don't quite trust it. Something is working—and maybe that's somehow more terrifying than when nothing was working. Things aren't going according to plan, but they're going somewhere interesting you didn't expect.

This is emergence. This is what happens when you stop trying to control every outcome and start working with what's unfolding.

For me (and maybe for you too) this part is uncomfortable. Growth doesn't feel like arrival. It feels like shedding old skin, and it can be painful. It feels like not knowing what comes next, like being visible in ways you're not sure you're ready for.

This section will help you recognize when to push forward and when to wait—and build momentum that doesn't burn you out.

The goal isn't just to get unstuck. The goal is to stay in motion without destroying yourself in the process.

What You'll Do

Navigate the discomfort of things working. Recognize when you're forcing vs. allowing. Decide when to persist and when to pivot. Build momentum that doesn't burn you out.

Time commitment: 1.5-2 hours, depending on your energy

What you'll need: Journal, pen, willingness to let things be messy

A Quick Note

If you've worked through the other sections, you might notice you're in new territory now. You've moved from thinking to doing. And doing can bring up all kinds of feelings.

That's what this section is for.

Emergence isn't neat. Usually doesn't follow your timeline and hardly ever looks like that vision board. It is real, and it's yours and you can choose to work with it instead of against it.

Let's figure out how.

Exercise 1: When Success Feels Scary

Energy Level: ✧ ✧   Time: 45 minutes

Why This Matters

You'd think success would feel good. You'd think that when things start working, you'd feel relief, excitement, validation.

Sometimes you do. But often, success is terrifying.

When things work, you become visible and outgrow old identities. There's no hiding behind "I'm trying" anymore. Now you're doing and your Inner Jerk shows up with her uninvited friend Impostor Syndrome (I know, how rude of them), and they have a field day.

This exercise helps you recognize the fear that shows up when things go right so you can stay in motion instead of sabotaging your own progress.

Part 1: What's Working?
Start by naming what's going well. This might feel uncomfortable. Do it anyway.

What's working in my life right now?
Be specific. What have you started? What's building momentum? What feels different than it did three months ago?

Example: I've been writing for months. I finished the final draft of this workbook. It's honestly something I never thought I could do. I'm creating new pieces and finally sorting out new and old mediums. I'm doing the things I kept saying I'd do 'someday.'

What surprised me about this?
What's going well that you didn't expect?
What surprised me:

Example: I'm surprised by how much I love the writing process when I'm not judging myself. I'm surprised that people are interested in my art. I'm surprised that pivoting away from a successful business felt like relief, not loss.

Part 2: What Fear Shows Up When Things Work?

Now the harder part. When things start working, what fears arise?

What scares me about things going well?
What thoughts show up when you acknowledge your progress?
What scares me about success:

> Example: I'm scared people will think I'm ridiculous for leaving my last business to make art and write books. I'm scared of being selfish—choosing creative work. I'm scared I'll invest all this time and energy and it won't work out. I'm scared I can't provide for my family this way.

What does my Inner Jerk say when things go well?
Listen to that critical voice. What does it say when you're succeeding?

> Example: Who do you think you are? You're terrible at this, you're too old for this. You can't make a living as an artist. What if you can't provide for your family? You're being irresponsible and selfish. You had a good thing and you walked away. What if this all falls apart and you have nothing?

What old identity am I outgrowing?
Who were you when you were stuck?
What's uncomfortable about becoming someone who's doing the thing?

**Old identity I'm leaving behind &
New identity I'm growing into:**

Example: *I've been playing small for years—the SAHM who dabbled in art but never fully committed to my dream. If I'm a working artist, I have to own that identity. I have to say 'I'm an artist' out loud without apologizing or explaining. This all feels scary and self-indulgent, even though I'm literally doing it.*

Part 3: The Pattern You're Breaking
If you've done I - Inner Inventory, you might recognize a pattern here. If not, that's okay—just answer honestly.

Have I sabotaged my own success before?
Think back. When things were going well in the past, what did you do?
How I've sabotaged before:

Example: Yes. I've convinced myself that creative work is a luxury, not a real pursuit. I've kept art as a 'someday' dream instead of making it my focus. Every creative project I've started, I've abandoned at 87% because taking them all the way felt too exposed.

What have I been protecting myself from by sabotaging?
There's always a reason. What have you been (or have in the past) avoiding by stopping?
What I've been protecting myself from:

Example: I've been protecting myself from the risk of visible failure, rejection, and from the responsibility of visible success. If I don't fully commit, I never have to find out if I'm good enough to make a living this way. I couldn't push past my fear of being seen, of failing publicly. But staying hidden isn't protecting me anymore.

What do I want to do differently this time?
What would it look like to stay in motion even when success feels scary?
    What I'm doing differently this time:

Example: *I want to notice the fear without letting it stop me. I want to keep writing and creating art even when my Inner Jerk says I'm being silly and selfish. I want to let people see this work even though that's scary. I want to say yes to showing up instead of hiding when things feel out of my control.*

Part 4: Staying With Success
Name the practices that will help you stay in motion when success brings up fear.

When I notice myself wanting to sabotage, I will:
Choose 1-2 practices that feel doable. My practices:

Example: I'll write down what my Inner Jerk is saying and then write what's true. I'll reach out to a friend instead of hiding. I'll take three deep breaths and ask myself—is this valuable feedback or fear? I'll say yes to one connection with my peeps even when hiding feels safer.

One truth I'm choosing to believe even (especially) when it feels uncomfortable:
What's the truth that will keep you moving forward?
The truth I'm choosing:

Example: I'm choosing to believe that creative work isn't selfish—it's finally taking myself seriously. I can provide for my family AND do work that brings me alive. Success doesn't have to mean constant hustle. My version of success is in line with how I work. Always on my terms.

I'll celebrate what's working instead of ignoring it:
How will you acknowledge your progress?
    How I'll celebrate:

    Example: *I'll keep a 'Let's GO' list. Every Friday, I'll write down one thing that worked—finishing a chapter, an hour in the darkroom, reaching out to a friend. Sharing something I'm working on. I won't minimize it. I'll just let it count.*

Exercise 2: Flow vs. Friction

Energy Level: ✧ ✧   Time: 30 minutes

Why This Matters

You've spent your whole life being told to hustle, push, make it happen. And sometimes that works. But just as often? Pushing creates friction.

Emergence requires a different skill, understanding when to act and when to wait. When to push and when to ease up. When to control and when to let go.

This exercise helps you recognize the difference between flow and friction so you can work with your natural rhythm instead of against it.

Part 1: The Difference Between Flow & Friction
Think about something you're currently working on—a project, a change or a new direction

What am I working on?

> Example: *I'm writing this workbook series, retreats and creating art for myself and collectors.*

When does this feel like flow?
When does the work feel easy, even if it's challenging?
When it feels like flow:

> Example: *It feels like flow when I'm writing in the morning. When I'm in the darkroom, a painting or when working on my sun prints. When I'm in conversation with people who get what I'm trying to create. Those parts feel great.*

When does this feel like friction?
When does it feel like you're pushing a boulder uphill?
When it feels like friction:

> Example: *It feels like friction when I try to work in ways that don't fit how I function. When I push myself into too much when I'm depleted. When I try to follow marketing advice that feels fake (or anything that feels fake). When I pull away completely and then force myself to be 'on' constantly to make up for it.*

Part 2: What Each One Is Telling You
Flow and friction are both giving you information. What are they telling you?

What does the flow tell me about my strengths and natural approach?
Where are you working with your gifts instead of against them? **What flow tells me:**

Example: Flow tells me I'm pretty good at creating meaningful work. I love writing when I give myself space to do it my way. I thrive in deep conversation and intimate gatherings. I'm good at creating experiences where people can explore what matters to them—no pretense, just good company and inspiration.

What does the friction tell me about what's not aligned?
Where are you trying to be someone you're not?
What friction tells me:

Example: Friction tells me I work best with both—time with people AND time alone to recharge. I can't force constant availability and I can't hide from everyone forever. I need both, and forcing either extreme breaks me.

Part 3: Adjusting Your Approach
Based on what flow and friction are telling you, what needs to shift?

What can I do more of that feels like flow?
Double down on what's working.
Mo' Flow:

Example: *I can write and share, and my work will find its people. I can create art that matters to me and show it to people. I can say yes to meaningful connections and no to draining obligations. I can say yes to connection when it feeds me and protect time alone when I need to recharge.*

What can I stop doing that creates friction?
Let go of what's not working.
Stop the friction:

Example: *I can stop trying to work in ways that don't fit me. I can stop hiding when I'm scared and then overcompensate by forcing myself into too much activity. I can stop comparing.*

Where can I ease up on control?
What could happen if I stopped forcing the timeline?
Easing up on control:

Example: *I can stop forcing results on my timeline. The book will matter to whoever it matters to—that's not mine to control. My art gets better the more I work, not the more I worry. I can honor my rhythm instead of forcing. Building slowly beats burning out.*

Exercise 3: The Pivot or Persist Decision

Energy Level: ✧ ✧   Time: 30 minutes

Why This Matters

At some point, you'll face this question—should I keep going or should I change direction?

This is one of the hardest decisions to make because we've been taught that quitting is failure and persistence is always noble. Welp, hate to break it to you...That's not true.

Sometimes persistence is courage. Sometimes it's stubbornness. Sometimes pivoting is wisdom. Sometimes it's fear.

This exercise helps you tell the difference so you can make the decision that serves you—not the decision that looks good or proves something to someone else.

Instructions:

Think about something you're doing where you're not sure whether to keep going or change course.

> **What am I considering pivoting away from?**
> **What I'm considering changing:**

> Example: *I've committed to being a working artist— writing books, creating art, hosting retreats. But I keep questioning if I'm being selfish by going all in on creative work when I need to help support my family financially.*

Why did I start this in the first place?
Connect back to your original motivation.
My original why:

> Example: *I wanted to do creative work that's mine. I want to build something around art and writing. I want to create work that helps people find their purpose again. And it starts with me walking the walk.*

Is that why still true for me?
Has what you want changed or remains the same?
Is my why still true:

> Example: *Yes—I still want creative work that matters. I'm terrified because this has to work. But that doesn't mean my why changed. It means I finally have to commit to it.*

What's the real feedback I'm getting?
Not your fear stories—actual information from doing the thing.
Real feedback:

> Example: *I'm making progress on the layout. The fear is loud. But this needs to be done so I can move on to making art and building the rest. The feedback is: finish it (get 'er done)*

What would need to change for this to feel aligned?
If you stayed, what would have to be different?
What would need to change:

> Example: *What I'm working on right now feels right. What needs to change is me actually committing and finishing. I need to stay present and share this even though it's scary.*

Is that change possible and worth it?
Can you make that shift? Do you want to?
Is it possible and worth it

> Example: *Yes and yes. Keeping my promise to myself to finish and share my work is possible. Putting my imperfect work out into the world is hard but doable. Worth it. (Cue Missy Elliott 'Work It', 2002)*

Am I pivoting because it's hard or because it's wrong?
There's a difference between hard-because-it's-new and hard-because-it's-misaligned.
Hard or wrong:

> Example: *It's hard because I'm scared and the pressure is real, not because it's wrong. The book feels right—it could help someone. My fear is about not being enough—not polished enough, not expert enough. But perfect keeps me small. I'd regret not trying more than any Inner Jerk criticism. Stay the course, as grandma would say.*

What does my gut say?
Underneath the fear and the "shoulds," what do you know?
What my gut knows:

> Example: *My gut says this is the way. My gut says my art and writing matter more than any business I've had before and I need to finish, share and connect with folks, even when (especially when) it's uncomfortable.*

The Decision Framework

Stay the Course if:

- ☐ The why still matters to you
- ☐ The hard parts are growing pains (fear, visibility, newness)
- ☐ It aligns with who you are and your values
- ☐ You're running from fear, not toward something better

Change direction if:

- ☐ The why has changed
- ☐ You're fighting against your natural strengths
- ☐ Real feedback says it's not working
- ☐ Continuing would require you to become someone you're not or going against your values

My decision & one action I'm taking based on this decision:

Example: I'm staying the course. (And if this book is in your hands, it means I followed through!) This week, I'm finishing the workbook and sharing my art. I'm reaching out to one person and sharing a work in progress (WIP) with them. Ready or not. And again, that's more than one thing, lol. eeeesh.

Exercise 4: Building Sustainable Momentum

Energy Level: ✧   Time: 20 minutes

Why This Matters

You know how to hustle. You know how to push through. Annnnddd you probably know how to burn yourself out in pursuit of a goal. That's not what you're doing this time.

This time, you're learning to build momentum that lasts. Some giddy-up that works with your life instead of against it. Momentum that doesn't require you to sacrifice your health, your relationships, or your sanity.

This exercise helps you identify what sustainable momentum looks like for you.

Instructions:

Answer these questions honestly. Not based on what you think you should do, but what works for you.

> **What's my natural rhythm?**
> Are you a sprint person or a steady-pace person? Morning or evening? Focused intensity or spread out over time?
> **My natural rhythm:**

> *Example: I'm a morning person (wasn't always, but my second-born had 4am plans for me for his first 4 years. He trained me well). I work best in focused blocks. I get distracted easily and task-switching kills my giddy-up and go. I thrive working my way—intense focus when the energy hits rather than consistent daily routines. I've made peace with that instead of fighting it.*

What do I need to maintain momentum without burning out? What supports your energy instead of draining it?
What I need:

Example: *I need morning creative time. I need time alone to recharge and time with people who get me. I need to say yes to my meaningful relationships and no to energy-draining obligations. I need to honor when I need to be alone and when I need to reach out.*

What does sustainable momentum feel like in my body? How do you know when you're in good momentum vs. burnout territory?
Sustainable momentum feels like:
Burnout feels like:

Example: *Sustainable momentum feels energized but not frantic. I sleep well. I have energy for other parts of my life. I feel engaged but not consumed. Burnout feels like pushing through exhaustion, sacrificing sleep, and getting irritable and icky with people I love.*

What are the early warning signs that I'm overdoing it?
How do you know when you're slipping into old patterns?
My warning signs:

> Example: I start hiding and convincing myself I don't need anyone. Or I overcommit and then crash hard. I start over-caffeinating and over-carbohydrating (that should be a word, JS). I stop creating. I start doubting everything and wonder if I'm being selfish. I get short with my family.

What's one practice that helps me stay in sustainable momentum? What keeps you balanced?
My practice:

> Example: Honoring how I work—reaching out when I need help, protecting time alone to recharge, and keeping my creative time sacred. Not forcing any of it.

This week, I will maintain momentum by
One small action that supports sustainable forward movement.
This week:

> Example: I'll protect my morning time to finish this book. That's it. FINISH. (and Share, y'all know by now just one is not my thang, do as I say...And all that.)

Integration: What I'm Taking Forward

Energy Level: ✧   Time: 15 minutes

Instructions:

You've explored what happens when things work, recognized where you experience flow vs. friction, decided between pivoting or staying the course, and identified how to build sustainable momentum.

Now, name what you're taking forward.

What I'm noticing about emergence and success feeling scary? What I'm noticing:

Example: I'm noticing that success can be more terrifying than failure because it makes me visible. I'm noticing that my Inner Jerk shows up loudest when things are working. I'm noticing that fear doesn't mean I'm on the wrong path—sometimes it just means I care. I'm noticing that staying in motion even when I'm scared works better than sabotaging my own progress at 87% complete.

Where am I experiencing flow? Where am I experiencing friction? My flow and friction:

Example: **Flow:** *Writing in the morning, working on new pieces, creating on my terms.*
Friction: *Following marketing advice (or anything) that feels fake, forcing myself into too much activity when I'm depleted. Comparing and endless ~~research~~ procrastination.*

My decision—persist or pivot?
What I've decided:

Example: *I'm staying the course. It's hard because sharing this and making it real feels scary. Possible rejection feels scary. The pressure to make this work is real. But it's not hard because it's wrong. My gut says this is the way. The book matters, my art matters. I'm finishing and sharing, ready or not.*

How I'm building momentum that lasts
Sustainable momentum looks like:

> Example: Working my way—intense focus when it hits, rest when I need it. Protecting my mornings. Reaching out when I need to, honoring time alone. Catching the warning signs before I crash. Finishing things instead of endless perfecting.

One action I'm taking this week.
This week:

> Example: I'm finishing this book. That's it. FINISH and share. Finish and share.

Closing Notes

Emergence is messy. It doesn't follow your plan and unfolds in ways you can't predict or control. That's exactly the point.

You're working with what's happening instead of your 'shoulds'. Staying in motion even when success feels scary. Recognizing the difference between forcing and easing up, between burning out and building sustainably.

This is what it looks like to stay unstuck. Not by controlling (ooofff, no likey) every outcome, but by staying present to what's unfolding and adjusting as you go.

You're doing this.

> **When Energy Is Low**
>
> ✧ Just do Exercise 4 (Building Sustainable Momentum) to reconnect with what sustainable forward movement feels like.
> ✧✧ Do Exercise 2 (Flow vs. Friction) to identify where you're working with your strengths vs. fighting against them.
> ✧✧✧ Complete Exercise 1 (When Success Feels Scary) when you have capacity for deeper reflection.

Keep on keepin' on. You've got this.

Jump to the next chapter (page 181): R - Review, Release & Rise, where you'll integrate everything you're noticing, celebrate how far you've come, and choose your next right thing forward into your next season.

Soup for the Season

Stumbling Into Something Good

You've done the work—recognizing when success feels scary, identifying flow vs. friction, keeping going even when uncomfortable. Now you need some soup that celebrates trying something new.

I was fishing (couldn't resist) for a better New England chowder recipe and stumbled upon Russ & Daughters' Lox Chowder. My searching suddenly stopped at 'Lox'—a born and raised New Yorker, later living in Alaska and the Olympic Peninsula, I'd somehow never heard of smoked salmon chowder.

Of course, this became a same-day must-try. My daughter (our family's soup snob and the same toddler from the *Tomorrow Dreaming Soup for the Season* page 145) gave it high praise. From an 18-year-old, impossible-to-impress young adult, I'm counting this as a big ol' W.

This is what embracing emergence looks like—stumbling onto something unexpected and trusting yourself to make it work

Credit where credit's due:

Russ & Daughters' Lox Chowder: https://www.saucemagazine.com/recipes/russ-and-daughters-lox-chowder-17368961

Sue Moran's Smoked Salmon Chowder: https://theviewfromgreatisland.com/smoked-salmon-chowder/

Smoked Salmon Chowda'

3	tablespoons extra-virgin olive oil, more for serving
1	large yellow onion, peeled and diced (2 cups)
4-8	large garlic cloves, chopped
2	medium carrots, chopped
2-3	celery stalks, chopped
1	cup diced potatoes
2	tablespoons vinegar
1/4	cup dry white wine or champagne (optional)
2	tablespoons "Better Than Bouillon" (Chicken or Veg)
4	cups water or broth
	Salt (if not using bouillon) or to taste
4-6	sprigs of thyme
2	bay leaves
1/2	cup (4 oz) cream cheese, cubed
4 oz	hot-smoked salmon
1	can/jar canned wild-caught salmon (remaining bones removed)
3	tablespoons fresh dill
	Fresh ground pepper & fresh dill, for serving

MAKE IT YOUR OWN:
Top with crispy bacon crumbles, homemade croutons, or both.
Add a dollop of sour cream or Greek yogurt.
Stir in corn kernels with the salmon.
Use leeks instead of onions for a sweeter flavor.
Add a pinch of smoked paprika or Old Bay seasoning.
Squeeze fresh lemon juice over individual bowls.
Serve with crusty bread for dipping. (HIGHLY Recommend this one!)

Step 1
Heat the oil over medium to high heat until warm. Stir in onion, celery, carrots, and potatoes; cook, stirring occasionally, until soft and golden brown, about 10 minutes. Stir in garlic and cook for 2 minutes.

Step 2
Stir in vinegar and wine to onion and garlic mixture. Using a wooden spoon, deglaze the pan, bringing up all those delicious golden brown bits into the liquid.

Step 3
Add 4 cups broth (or water) to the pot. Stir in the bouillon until it dissolves. Add salt if not using bouillon, or season to taste. Add fresh thyme and bay leaves. Bring mixture to a simmer and cook, uncovered, 5 minutes. Lower heat to medium-low and cook about 20 minutes.

Step 4
Reduce heat to low. Add cream cheese cubes and stir until melted and fully incorporated into the broth, about 3-5 minutes.

Step 5
Flake both the hot-smoked salmon and canned salmon into soup and stir in fresh dill. Return the soup to the heat to warm through. Top with fresh ground pepper and sprinkle with some fresh dill.

Review, Release, & Rise

> "Into a daybreak that's wondrously clear
> I rise..."
>
> —Maya Angelou, from "Still I Rise"

REVIEW, RELEASE & RISE|
INTEGRATION & MOVING FORWARD

You've done the hard work. You know what matters to you (W), understand your patterns (I), and gotten brutally honest about where you are (N). You're dreaming of what's possible again (T) and practiced working with what's emerging (E).

Now it's time to look back at where you've been, see how far you've come, and decide what's next.

This section pulls together everything you've done so you can choose how you want to move forward. You don't need all the answers—just recognize what's shifted, release what no longer serves you, and take one clear step toward what does. You don't have to have it all figured out. You just need to know your next right thing.

Why This Matters

Being stuck isn't just about being unable to move forward—it's also about not recognizing when you already have.

You've been working through this workbook—noticing, shifting, trying new things. You've been trusting yourself instead of outsourcing every answer. But if you don't pause to see what's changed, you'll miss the proof that you're no longer stuck.

This section helps you see your progress, make peace with what didn't work, and get clear on what comes next. Not five years from now—just the next right thing.

Staying stuck often means staying blind to how far you've already come.

What You'll Do

See how far you've come. Release what no longer serves you. Name what's different. Choose your next right thing.

Time commitment: 1.5-2 hours, depending on your energy

What you'll need: Journal, pen, all your previous work from W, I, N, T, and E (if you did them)

Exercise 1: The Evidence Review ✧ ✧
Look back at the patterns you identified in the Inner Inventory section and see what's shifted.

Exercise 2: The Release ✧ ✧ ✧
Decide what's worth keeping and what you're ready to release.

Exercise 3: Your RISE Statement ✧ ✧
Get clear on the one thing you're committing to do next.

Exercise 4: The Next Season ✧ ✧
Identify your 90-day commitment and how you'll support yourself.

Integration: Wrapping It All Up ✧
What you're taking forward and what you're leaving behind.

A Quick Note

If you jumped straight to this section because you're ready to move forward, welcome. You can start here if you've already done the heavy lifting on your own—just focus on where you are right now and what you're ready to release and choose next.

If you've worked through the other sections, you've shown up for yourself in a big way. This is where you see how far you've come. Where you name what's different. Where you choose what comes next.

This is where you see what's working, let go of what's not, and choose what comes next. On your terms.

Exercise 1: The Evidence Review
Energy Level: ✧ ✧   Time: 30 minutes

Why This Matters

When you're in the middle of it, you can't see how far you've come. You're too busy watching what's not done yet, what's still hard, how far you still have to go.

This exercise makes you look at the proof—what's changed, what shifted, what's different now.

You did the work. Look at what it did.

Instructions:
Go back through your work in W, I, N, T, and E. If you didn't complete all the sections, look back on your own experiences that align with the prompts below. If you journal regularly, review those entries.

For each section, answer these questions:

W - Wisdom Gathering
What do you now know about what matters to you?
What I now know about my values:

Example: *I now know that I value making over status. That I've been living someone else's version of a good life. I now know that rest isn't optional—it's required.*

I - Inner Inventory
What do you now know about your patterns?
What I now know about my patterns:

Example: *I now know that I sabotage myself right before success because success feels scarier than staying small. That my Inner Jerk sometimes sounds exactly like my abusive ex from my teen years. That I've been 'calling it in' for years instead of fully committing to what I want.*

N - Now Moment
What do you now know about where you actually are?
What I now know about my current reality:

> Example: *I now know that I've been lying to myself about how 'fine' everything is. That the gap between my values and my life is bigger than I wanted to admit. That I have more resources than I've been acknowledging.*

T - Tomorrow Dreaming
What do you now know about what's possible?
What I now know about possibility:

> Example: *I now know that I'm allowed to want what I want without apologizing. That starting over in my 50s isn't a crisis—it's brave. That the smallest versions of my dreams still matter. That my version of success never looks like I thought it would.*

E - Embracing Emergence
What do you now know about working with what's unfolding?
What I now know about emergence:

> Example: *I now know that success can feel scarier than failure. That I work best when I have the freedom to do it my way, and that looks different from how everyone else works.*

The Big Picture

Looking at all your answers, what's the through-line? What theme or truth keeps showing up across multiple sections?

My through-line:

> Example: *I've been playing small, some part of me thinking that's how I stay safe, but staying small and hidden has kept me stuck. I'm ready to be seen even though it's uncomfortable.*

What's one thing you know now that you didn't know when you started?
What I know now:

> Example: *I know now that I'm not broken. I was just trying to live a life that doesn't fit me anymore.*

What surprised you most as you looked back through your work?
What surprised me:

Example: I *was surprised by how many small shifts I'd already made without realizing it. Looks like I've been moving forward slooowwly, but moving.*

What's different about you now compared to when you started WINTER?
Be specific. What have you done?
What have you stopped doing?
How do you show up differently?
What's different now:

Example: *I'm protecting my creative time. I finished this book. I'm building the Wintering Well retreat for February 2026. I'm creating instead of just planning to create someday.*

Note: There's a Release Ritual in the Ritual section that pairs with the following exercise on page 22. You can do that ritual, or create your own—burn it, bury it, rip it up, whatever feels right. The point is to make it physical and real.

Exercise 2: The Release
Energy Level: ✧ ✧ ✧   Time: 45 minutes

Why This Matters

Life has a funny way of teaching us. The tighter you grip what used to work, the less room you have for what might work better for you now.

You can't step into who you're becoming while dragging everything you were. At some point, you have to look at what you're carrying and decide what's worth the weight and what needs to be let go.

Release isn't about erasing your past or pretending it didn't happen. It's about acknowledging what served you once but doesn't serve you now—and choosing to let it go.

This exercise helps you name what you're releasing so you can, well...Release it. Not just in your head (we're all guilty of that)—physically and emotionally too. Knowing you should let something go and letting it go are two completely different things.

Part 1: What I'm Releasing
Instructions:
Name what you're actively choosing to release. Be specific.

Old identities I'm releasing
Who were you that you're no longer choosing to be?

> Example: I'm releasing the identity of 'the know-it-all' who had to have all the answers. I'm releasing the version of me who equated busy with worthy. I'm releasing the identity of someone who calls it in instead of fully committing.

Old stories I'm releasing
What narratives about yourself are you done believing?

> Example: I'm releasing the story that I'm too old to start over. I'm releasing the story that creative work is selfish. I'm releasing the story that pursuing what I want means failing the people I love.

Old patterns I'm releasing
What behaviors or habits are you done repeating?

Example: *I'm releasing the pattern of sabotaging myself right before success. I'm releasing the pattern of hiding when I'm scared. I'm releasing the pattern of starting things and not finishing them.*

Old fears I'm releasing
What are you done letting fear dictate?

Example: *I'm releasing the fear that success means I'm still a target and everything will be stolen from me again. I'm releasing the fear that I'm not good enough. I'm releasing the fear that it's too late for me.*

Part 2: Why I'm Releasing This

Instructions:
For each thing you're releasing, name why.
What has holding onto this cost you?

Pick your top 3 releases (the ones that feel most important) and answer:

Release #1:

What I'm releasing:

What holding onto this has cost me:

Example: *The know-it-all identity has kept me isolated and exhausted trying to have all the answers. 'Busy equals worthy' has cost me years of rest, my health, and the ability to enjoy making things. Endless procrastination and perfecting instead of creating and sharing.*

Release #2:

What I'm releasing:

What holding onto this has cost me:

Release #3:

What I'm releasing:

What holding onto this has cost me:

Part 3: What I'm Choosing Instead

Instructions:
Release creates space. What are you choosing in that space?

Instead of the old identity, I'm choosing:

Example: *Instead of 'the know-it-all,' I'm choosing to be a beginner who asks questions. Instead of 'busy equals worthy,' I'm choosing to rest without guilt and to create without grinding.*

Instead of the old story, I'm choosing:

Example: *Instead of 'too old to start over,' I'm choosing to build what I need in my 50s. Instead of 'art is selfish,' I'm choosing to show up for my work—the darkroom, the writing, the retreats—without apologizing.*

Instead of the old pattern, I'm choosing:

Example: *Instead of sabotaging before success, I'm choosing to keep going even when it's uncomfortable. Instead of hiding when scared, I'm choosing to reach out when I need to.*

Instead of the old fear, I'm choosing:

Example: *Instead of fearing success will spiral out of control, I'm choosing to believe I can handle what comes. Instead of fearing I'm not good enough, I'm choosing to look at the evidence that I'm already doing it.*

The Release Practice

Use the following page to write what you're releasing. Then tear it out and complete your ritual.

> Make this release physical and real.
> Do the ritual from this book on page 22, create your own, write it down and burn it, rip it up, bury it—whatever feels right.
>
> **My release practice:**
>
>
>
>
>
> Example: *I'm going to write everything I'm releasing on paper, read it out loud, thank it for what it taught me, and then burn it. I'll scatter the ashes in the garden and plant something special there.*
>
> **When will you do this?**
> Put a date on it. Make it real.

Exercise 3: Your RISE Statement
Energy Level: ✧ ✧   Time: 15 minutes

Why This Matters

You just need to know what comes next. Not the whole path—just the next step.

This exercise helps you get clear on your next right thing— the one action, decision, or step that moves you forward from where you are right now.

Not someday. Not eventually. Next.

Instructions:
This exercise walks you through creating your RISE statement—your declaration of what comes next. You'll answer a series of questions, then pull it all together into one clear commitment at the end.

After all the work you've done in W, I, N, T, and E—what keeps nagging at you? What idea, project, or change keeps showing up no matter how many times you push it away?

What keeps nagging at me:

Example: *The workbook keeps showing up in my journaling. The Ireland and UK retreat ideas surface every time I dream about what's next. The darkroom sits there waiting—I can't stop thinking about getting back in there.*

Based on everything you've done in this workbook. **What's the one thing you're committing to do next?**

Example: *Finish this workbook and get it published.*

Why does this matter?

Example: *Finishing the workbook will give me proof that I can complete something. Getting it published makes it real—not just another project sitting at mostly done.*

What might get in your way, and how will you handle it?

Example: *My 87% pattern will show up. When it does, I'll remember that done matters more than perfect. Jory the Jerk will tell me no one cares—I'll thank her for trying to protect me and keep working anyway.*

REVIEW, RELEASE & RISE

When will you start? Put a date and time on it.

My RISE statement:
Write it out. Make it real.

Example: I commit to finishing the layout of this workbook by the end of this week. I commit to showing up even when it's hard, to finishing instead of stopping at 87%. My creative work isn't selfish—it matters. This is my next right thing, and I'm doing it.

Exercise 4: The Next Season
Energy Level: ✧ ✧   **Time: 20 minutes**

Why This Matters

You did the review and made your declaration. That's great—but declarations don't mean much without action.

I've found, goals set too far out tend not to work. One to five-year plans—that's way too far out. Too much changes. You lose momentum, life happens, the goal becomes irrelevant. Ninety days is short enough to stay focused (even for my messy mind) and long enough to see legit change.

This exercise makes your commitment concrete. What are you doing for the next 90 days? How will you support yourself? What happens when you start to slip?

Not forever. Just the next 90 days.

Instructions:
Answer these questions quickly. Don't overthink.

What's one thing I'm committing to for the next 90 days?
Be specific. Make it doable from where you are.
My 90-day commitment:

Example: I'm committing to finishing and publishing this book in the next 90 days—which means finishing the proof, setting up pre-orders, and getting it out there. Let's GO!

What would make this easier?
What support, structure, or boundary would help you keep this commitment?
What would help:

Example: Telling my family that my mornings are non-negotiable. Setting up my workspace the night before. Checking in with a friend weekly to stay accountable. Working my way instead of trying to force it.

What's my early warning sign that I'm slipping back into old patterns?
How will you know when you're losing momentum?
My warning sign:

Example: I start hiding. I stop creating and switch to 'research' or I start changing the plan again. I start chugging copious amounts of coffee and crappy carbs. I get short with my family. I tell myself I'll start tomorrow.

What will I do when I notice that warning sign?
Have a plan for when the pattern shows up.
My response:

Example: I'll reach out to one friend instead of hiding. I'll start creating even if I don't feel inspired. I'll read my RISE Statement and remind myself why I'm doing this.

Who am I asking to support me?
You don't have to do this alone. Who can you ask?
Who I'm asking:

> Example: *I'm asking my Mr. to help so I can protect my morning time. I'll check in with my sisters every Friday. I'll schedule some time on that body doubling app I've been meaning to try.*

How will I know this season was successful?
What will be different 90 days from now if you honor this commitment?
Success looks like:

> Example: *The book will be published. I'll be working in the darkroom regularly instead of just planning to. I'll have finished and shared my work. I'll have proof that I can finish what I start.*

Integration: Wrapping it All Up

Energy Level: ✦   Time: 15 minutes

Instructions:
You've reviewed, released, and risen. Time to wrap it up—we're keeping it simple and sweet. When you're ready, you'll be stepping into the next season on your own terms.

Answer these last questions:

> **My through-line across WINTER**
> What truth kept showing up throughout this whole journey?

My through-line:

> Example: *I've been playing small, some part of me thinking that's how I stay safe, but staying small and hidden has kept me stuck. I'm ready to be seen even though it's uncomfortable.*

What I'm taking forward
What are you carrying into the next season?

What I'm taking forward:

> Example: *I'm taking forward that I need to share my work, not just make it. I'm taking forward the proof that I can finish what I start—this workbook is evidence. I'm taking forward the knowledge that hiding when scared doesn't serve me.*

What I'm leaving behind
What are you done dragging with you?

What I'm leaving behind:

Example: *I'm leaving behind the story that my art and writing are selfish. I'm done apologizing for what matters to me.*

My commitment to myself for the next season:
What's the promise you're making?

My commitment:

Example: *I commit to finishing and publishing this workbook. When I've honored that promise, I'll start the Ireland retreat and Book 2. I commit to asking for help when I'm scared.*

Closing Notes

You showed up and did the work. You looked at the hard shhhtuff, named what matters most, released what doesn't, and chose who you're becoming.

This isn't the end. This is the completion of one cycle so you can begin the next. Please, come back to WINTER whenever you need it. Know that savoring the cozy quiet and stillness is not the same as stuck. It's Wintering Well.

That's what WINTER is really about. Remembering who you are underneath all the stories and patterns and fears. Rediscovering the best parts of yourself is you choosing yourself.

You're not starting from scratch. You're starting from here.

That's more than enough. You're more than enough. (I get to be cheesy; we're nearing the end of our time together here.)

Watch for it in the days and weeks ahead—movement, momentum, the feeling of being unstuck. Even if it's small or a little (a lot) scary. Even if it's barely noticeable. It counts. Celebrate it.

Old patterns will show back up. They always do. When they do, come back here. Remember what you uncovered about yourself here. Choose yourself again, and again, and again.

Right now tho', celebrate you. You did something most people never do—you looked at what wasn't working and you've chosen to do something about it. You showed up for yourself. Way to go. I'm sending you a squeeze—you should be proud of yourself, and know that I'm proud of you too.

When you're ready, go build what's yours. Show up for what matters most.

The next season will be there whenever you're ready.

But first—take a breath, rest annnd then—celebrate!

Keep choosing you. That's how you rise.

When Energy Is Low

- ✧ Just do Exercise 4 (The Next Season) to identify your one next commitment
- ✧✧ Do Exercises 1 & 3 (Evidence Review and RISE Statement) to see how far you've come
- ✧✧✧ Complete all exercises when you have capacity for deeper integration

You did it. YAAAYYYY!

REVIEW, RELEASE & RISE

Soup for the Season

Full Circle—Coming Home to Yourself

You've reviewed your journey and released what no longer serves you. Time for something that brings you full circle. Back to beautiful basics—classic, grounding, and deeply satisfying

This beef stew is where it all comes together. You have the foundation (stock from W). You have the technique (building layers from I, N, T, E). Now you trust yourself enough to make it your own. Add what feels right. Adjust to your taste. This is intuitive cooking—which is really just trusting yourself.

Credit where credit's due: Molly O'Neill (1952-2019)

I don't think I've ever had a food writer make me tear up. I tracked this recipe back to Ms. O'Neill's 1994 article "A Simmer of Hope"—and boy, could we use a big bowl of that these days (serious sigh). And then I found out she's my all-time favorite Yankee's big sister. True story.

> A few sentences into the article she said this perfection: "Outside the kitchen, to stew is to fret, to be vexed and worried, to fall victim to your own actions. In the kitchen, however, to stew is to hope—to hope that the choice of ingredients will meld felicitously as they mellow together in a pot. Instinct is needed to season properly..."

Old Fashioned Beef Stew

¼	cup all-purpose flour
¼	teaspoon freshly ground pepper
1	pound beef stewing meat, trimmed and cut into inch cubes
5	teaspoons vegetable oil
2	tablespoons red wine vinegar
1	cup red wine
3½	cups beef broth
2	bay leaves
1	medium onion, peeled and chopped
5	medium carrots, peeled and cut into ¼-inch rounds
2	large baking potatoes, peeled and cut into ¾-inch cubes
2	teaspoons salt

YOUR SPECIAL TOUCHES:
You've spent this whole workbook learning to trust yourself. Here's where you practice. Add what sounds good. Skip what doesn't. Season by instinct.
Make this stew yours.

Make It Your Own:
Add mushrooms if you want earthiness. Swap potatoes for parsnips. Use Guinness instead of wine (if you want my famous Guinness beef stew recipe, reach out—I'm happy to share). Add herbs that call to you. You know what sounds good.

Step 1
Combine the flour and pepper in a bowl, add the beef and toss to coat well. Heat 3 teaspoons of the oil in a large pot. Add the beef a few pieces at a time; do not overcrowd. Cook, turning the pieces until beef is browned on all sides, about 5 minutes per batch; add more oil as needed between batches.

Step 2
Remove the beef from the pot and add the vinegar and wine. Cook over medium-high heat, scraping the pan with a wooden spoon to loosen any browned bits. Add the beef, beef broth, and bay leaves. Bring to a boil, then reduce to a slow simmer.

Step 3
Cover and cook, skimming broth from time to time, until the beef is tender, about 1½ hours. Add the onions and carrots and simmer, covered, for 10 minutes. Add the potatoes and simmer until vegetables are tender, about 30 minutes more. Add broth or water if the stew is dry. Season with salt and pepper to taste. Ladle among 4 bowls and serve.

Welp, you've come full circle. From making stock to trusting yourself to season by instinct. From following structured recipes to creating your own. From building foundations to trusting yourself.

This is what the whole WINTER journey has been about—building the foundation, examining the patterns, getting honest about where you are, envisioning what's possible, embracing what emerges, and integrating it all.

Now you know how to make soul-soothing soups. In the kitchen and in life.

Trust your instincts. Season to taste. Make it yours.

CLOSING: CARRYING WINTER FORWARD

You made it.

You might have worked through every section in order, or jumped around doing only what called to you. Maybe you're still working through some sections and just wanted to peek at the ending. Doesn't matter.

However you got here—you showed up.

What You Did

You did the hard work, you put the *work* in this workbook. (I digress—I can no longer contain my inner cornball—release the puns)

You've done the work. You're getting unstuck.

I wish this was one and done, but y'all know life doesn't work that way. We'll winter again. There'll be a different season, different place, different wisdom to gather. When it's time to start again—and again—we know where to look. We'll know that we've done it before and we can do it again.

What You Know Now

Stuck isn't failure—it's your signal to start noticing.

Your way of doing things (the spirals, the twirls, the non-linear path, the rebellious resistance to routines) isn't broken. It's yours.

Starting over at any age isn't a crisis. It's courage.

The smallest versions of your dreams still matter, and progress is never linear. Finishing even one thing proves you can finish anything.

Most importantly, you can trust yourself to find your way through the dark—even when every part of you is screaming to quit.

What You're Carrying Forward

You don't need to leave any of this behind. These were hard-fought battles. You carry this wisdom with you into all your seasons.

When you find yourself stuck again (and you will), you'll know what to do. Light a candle. Return to your values. Get honest about where you are. Start with the smallest version of your dream. Take your next step. Say yes to connection Ask for help instead of white-knuckling it alone.

You have what you need now. You have proof that you can do hard things—you always could.

What Comes Next

This workbook is the first of four in the Seasons of Wisdom Series (it's a working title, I'm open to suggestions if you have 'em?). You've built the foundation—the part about refusing to disappear and finding your way back to yourself. The other books explore the seasons that follow—emerging in spring, sustaining through summer, harvesting in autumn

Right now, you're standing on solid ground. You have what you need.

What matters, your patterns, where you want to go—you know these things now. You can trust yourself and hush your Inner Jerk when she shows up. She will. You know how to work with what emerges instead of forcing outcomes you can't control.

That's more than enough to begin again, for as many times as you need to begin again.

One Last Thing

You don't have to have it all figured out. Perfect is just an excuse to stay small. Your life, your way, always.

You simply have to keep showing up. Keep choosing you. Keep building from where you are and not from where you think you should be.

Winter is just the beginning of your newest story. It's the slow stretch where you remember who you are underneath all the noise, all the "shoulds," all the borrowed expectations—and then, you choose to live from that truth.

You're not broken. You were never broken.

You're just someone who needed a little Wintering Well.

The momentum is yours. You're ready.

Go. Build what's yours. Live what's true. Show up for what matters.

One season at a time. The next one is waiting.

And you're ready for whatever awaits.

—Chandra

CLOSING: CARRYING WINTER FORWARD

Acknowledgements

A special note of gratitude.

ACKNOWLEDGMENTS

To my Mr.—thank you for your unwavering love and support over the last 20+ years, but especially these last few. For this family, home and life filled with laughter, love and light. There is no timeline I would rather be on than on this one with you.
Love you today, through all of our tomorrows and beyond.

To my Kids—thank you for being your most amazing selves. For showing up every day with joy and staggering strength even when life gets challenging. I've learned so much from you. It's the honor of my life to be your mom. I hope many years from now you can see this book and always remember, it's never too late to start again.

To my Parents—thank you for your truly unconditional love, support and strength, for showing us that 'there's always a way' and for never making me feel like I had to do things any other way but my own. You're the champions who taught us that integrity, honor and kindness are the only way. You are the strongest, most caring people I know. Grateful for every moment knowing that I won the family lotto being born to you.

To my Brother—wherever you may roam, sailing amongst the stars— It's your light that gets me back up every single time I'm knocked down. You are missed, big brother. You are loved.

To my Sisters & my Biddies who never disappear when I go into my hidey hole—thank you for always showing up even when I try my best to be invisible. For checking in. For understanding.
For seeing me. You know who you are.

> To every person who's ever felt stuck & wondered
> if there was another way—this is for you.
> Thank you for trusting me with your winters.

And to Me (y'all know I had to—ha!) for getting out of my own way (again), for not giving up even when every part of me was screaming to quit. For committing to finish and share the questions & challenges that became this book—ya done good, kid.

INDEX

JUMP TO WHAT YOU NEED

Finding What You Need

Use this guide to jump directly to exercises based on your current energy level or what you're feeling right now.

BY ENERGY LEVEL

When Energy Is Low (✧ Exercises)

W - Wisdom Gathering Exercise 1:
    First Scan—What Lights You Up?
    Just circle values that resonate—skip the rest
	29

I - Inner Inventory *Just name your Inner Jerk's top 3 phrases*	80

N - Now Moment Exercise 4:
    Your Resources
    Ground yourself in what you actually have
	114

T - Tomorrow Dreaming Exercise 4:
    What If It Works?
    Practice imagining success instead of catastrophizing
	138

E - Embracing Emergence Exercise 4:
    Sustainable Momentum Reconnect with what
    sustainable fwd. movement feels like
	170

R - Review, Release & Rise Exercise 4: The Next Season Identify your one next commitment	202

INDEX

When You Have Medium Energy (✧✧ Exercises)

W - Wisdom Gathering Exercise 2: Real vs. Should Test 32
　　　　　　　　　　　Exercise 3: Body Wisdom Check 36

I - Inner Inventory Exercise 1: Where Values Come From? 63
　　　　　　　　　　　Exercise 2: What Keeps Repeating? 72

N - Now Moment Exercise 1: The Truth Snapshot 98
　　　　　　　　　　　Exercise 2: Stories vs. Reality 106

T - Tomorrow Dreaming Exercise 2: 6-Month Snapshot 134

E - Embracing Emergence Exercise 2: Flow vs. Friction 160
　　　　　　　　　　　Exercise 3: Pivot or Persist 165

R - Review, Release & Rise Exercise 1: Evidence Review 184
　　　　　　　　　　　Exercise 3: Rise Statement 199

When You Have Capacity to Go Deep (✧✧✧ Exercises)

W - Wisdom Gathering Exercise 4: Shadow Awareness 45

I - Inner Inventory Exercise 3: Peace with Your Inner Jerk 80

N - Now Moment Exercise 3: The Anxiety/Regret Audit 110

T - Tomorrow Dreaming Exercise 1: What Do You Want? 128

E - Emergence Exercise 1: When Success Feels Scary 152

R - Review, Release & Rise Exercise 2: The Release 189

INDEX

BY WHAT YOU'RE FEELING

When you're feeling lost or unclear about what matters
➻ Start with W - Wisdom Gathering　　　　　　　　27
Reconnect with your core values and what actually matters to you

When you keep repeating the same patterns
➻ Start with I - Inner Inventory, Exercise 2　　　　72
Identify what keeps you stuck and why

When your Inner Jerk is loud and mean
➻ Start with I - Inner Inventory, Exercise 3　　　　80
Make peace with that critical voice

When you're overwhelmed by everything
➻ Start with N - Now Moment, Exercise 4　　　　114
Ground yourself in what you actually have right now

When you can't see the gap between your values and your reality
➻ Start with N - Now Moment, Exercise 1　　　　98
Take an honest snapshot of where you actually are

When you're stuck in the past or anxious about the future
➻ Start with N - Now Moment, Exercise 3　　　　110
Bring yourself back to the present

When you've forgotten how to dream
➻ Start with T - Tomorrow Dreaming　　　　　　125
Imagine what's possible

INDEX

When your dreams feel too big and overwhelming
↠ Start with T - Tomorrow Dreaming, Exercise 3   138
Find the smallest version that still matters

When success feels scary
↠ Start with E - Embracing Emergence, Exercise 1   152
Navigate the discomfort of things actually working

When you're forcing instead of allowing
↠ Start with E - Embracing Emergence, Exercise 2   160
Recognize when you're working with your
strengths vs. fighting against them

When you don't know whether to keep going or change direction
↠ Start with E - Embracing Emergence, Exercise 3   165
Decide when to persist and when to pivot

When you're burning out
↠ Start with E - Embracing Emergence, Exercise 4   170
Build momentum that doesn't destroy you

When you're ready to integrate everything and move forward
↠ Start with R - Review, Release & Rise   181
See how far you've come and claim who you're becoming

INDEX

BY SOUP FOR THE SEASON

When you need to build your foundation
➻ W - Taking Stock: Stocks　　　　　　　　　　58
Vegetable or Chicken stock—the foundation
for everything that follows

When you're examining your layers
➻ I - Foundations Mushroom Stew　　　　　　92
Building complexity on your foundation

When you need clarity and grounding
➻ N - Clarity Carrot Soup　　　　　　　　　　122
Bright, nourishing, with room to adapt

When you're creating from what you have

➻ T - Tomorrow Tomato Bisque　　　　　　　146
Born from necessity, made with what's available

When you're trying something new
➻ E - Smoked Salmon Chowda'　　　　　　　178
Stumbling into something unexpected and good

When you're coming full circle
➻ R - Old Fashioned Beef Stew　　　　　　　212
Trusting yourself to season by instinct

See complete Soup for the Season Index on page 226 for all recipes

INDEX

BY RITUAL / CEREMONY

When you want to mark transitions with intention:

➻ Winter Rituals Overview — 12
➻ W - Wisdom Gathering: The Opening Light — 16
➻ I - Inner Inventory: Mirror Moment — 17
➻ N - Now Moment: Grounding Practice — 18
➻ T - Tomorrow Dreaming: Vision Setting — 19
➻ E - Embracing Emergence: Threshold Step — 20
➻ R - Review, Release & Rise: Letting Go — 22

SOUP FOR THE SEASON INDEX
All Recipes at a Glance

Each WINTER section includes a recipe that mirrors the work you're doing. Here's where to find them all.

W - Wisdom Gathering
Taking Stock: Stocks   56
Building your foundation from scratch
Vegetable Stock & Chicken Stock
Credit: Dana Monsees (stock vs broth explanation)

I - Inner Inventory
Memories Mushroom Stew   91
Building on your foundation with layers and depth

N - Now Moment
Zesty Clarity Carrot Soup   121
Bright, nourishing, and grounding—with room to adapt
Credit: Based on Melissa Clark's Carrot and Cauliflower Soup

INDEX

T - Tomorrow Dreaming
Tomorrow Tomato Bisque   145
Credit: This one is Chandra's own through and through

E - Embracing Emergence
Smoked Salmon Chowda'   177
Credit: Russ & Daughters' Lox Chowder and Sue Moran's
Smoked Salmon Chowder

R - Review, Release & Rise   211
Old Fashioned Beef Stew
Full circle—coming home to yourself with intuitive cooking
Credit: Molly O'Neill, from "A Simmer of Hope" (1994)

About the Recipes

These recipes are designed to be flexible. Substitute ingredients. Adjust seasonings. Make them your own. The measurements are guides, not rules.

Freezing soups and stocks: Most of these freeze beautifully for up to 3 months. Perfect for low-energy days when you need nourishment without effort.

Making your own stock: Once you learn to make stock (W section), you'll use it throughout the other recipes. It's the foundation everything else builds on—just like the work in this book.

CURIOSITIES & COMPANIONS
Books, Podcasts, People & Wisdom Worth Exploring

Katherine May
Wintering:
The Power of Rest
and Retreat...
katherine-may.co.uk
@katherinemay_

ERFAHRUNGSRAUM

Campbell Walker
Your Head is a
Houseboat
Doom & Bloom
struthless.com
@struthless69

Amie McNee
We Need Your Art:
Stop Messing Around
and Make Something
amiemcnee.com
@inspiredtowrite

Pamela Colman
Smith
Alone
RWS Deck, Letters
& Art

Henry Miller
On Turning Eighty
On Writing

Carlo Rovelli

Sharon Blackie
Hagitude
sharonblackie.net
hagitude.org
@sharonblackie-
mythmakings

Maya Angelou
Caged Bird
And Still I Rise

Rose Macaulay
What Not

ANKOSÉ

Edmonia Lewis

Epictetus

Paul Robeson
Here I Stand

Thomas Paine
Common Sense

Elsa Pederson
The Katchemak Bay
Years

Antoine de
Saint-Exupéry
The Little Prince

John Berger
Ways of Seeing

Wendell Berry *The*
Peace of Wild Things:
And Other Poems
Our Real Work
How to Be a Poet
berrycenter.org

Albert Kahn
The Archives of the
Planet

Fannie Lou Hamer

Frederick Frank
What Matters

SEANCHAS

Laurence Shames &
Peter Barton
Not Fade Away: A
Short Life Well Lived

Billie Holiday
Strange Fruit

Eugene Field
The Love Affairs of a
Bibliomaniac

Edward Everette
Hale
The Man Without A
Country

Albert Einstein

CURIOSITIES & COMPANIONS

Molly O'Neill
American Food Writing: An Anthology

TĀ-VĀ

Margaret Macdonald Mackintosh
Pool of Silence
The May Queen & *The Wassail* by her Hubs

Maria Popova
An Almanac of Birds: 100 Divinations...
TheMarginalian.com

Christy Mandin
Millie Fleur's Poison Garden
@christymandin

Elisabet Ney

Luke Adam Hawker
The Last Tree
@lukeadamhawker

DAO

Krista Tippett
On Being podcast & Productions
onbeing.org

KALA and **MANA**

Charlie Mackesy
The Boy, The Mole, The Fox And The Horse
charliemackesy.com
@charliemackes

Mitákuye Oyás'iŋ

Robert Frank
The Americans
Art

Brooks Jensen
LensWork podcast
lenswork.com
brooksjensenarts.com

CODDIWOMPLE

J. Sybylla Smith
Concept Aware
jsybyllasmith.com
@jsybylla

Ibarionex Perrello
The Candid Frame podcast & art
ibarionex.net
@ibarionex

Joanna (J.F.) Penn
The Creative Penn
thecreativepenn.com
@jfpennauthor

David McRaney
You Are Not So Smart (pod & books)
davidmcraney.com

Kate Chadbourne
katechadbourne.com

Erwartungshorizont

Florestine Perrault Collins
Gertrude Käsebier
Berenice Abbot
Josef Sudek
Edward Weston
Aperture
The Harry Ransom Center (ATX)
The Cloisters (NYC)

This is a very, very short ever-growing (like by the second) list of my current obsessions, curiosities, admiration and inspirations. **M**y go-to LLMs for research and editing are Gemini and Claude. **A**nnnd now it's your turn. As always, your public library (if you have access) and the Internet Archive (Archive.org) are fab places for your own treasure hunting.

A FINAL INVITATION

If this book helped you find your way through your own winter, I'd love to hear about it.

Not because I need validation (well, maybe a little), but because knowing it helped makes all the hard work of sharing it worth it.

Stay Connected

Join the Solstice & Stone community for more seasonal wisdom, workshops, and retreats:

Website: solstice-stone.com
Instagram: @solstice_stone
Free Book Club: bookclub.solstice-stone.com

Email: hello@solstice-stone.com

Share your story using #WinteringWell and #RefuseToDisappear

Tell a friend who's stuck.

We're all just figuring this out as we go. But we don't have to figure it out alone.

Winter well, my friend.

—Chandra

ABOUT THE AUTHOR

Chandra Achberger is a lifelong maker and artist who creates with 100-year-old cameras, expired film and papers, and darkroom chemicals brewed from wildflowers, weeds, and garden scraps. She's been making things since she was three—fashion design and darkroom photography since middle school, with detours through sculpture and art history along the way.

At 50, after over two decades of navigating grief, depression, cPTSD, and complete financial ruin after a series of unfortunate events and a failed international move—she wrote her way through it. The WINTER method came from a desperate 100-day challenge she created for herself: no bread, no booze, no sugar, walking miles every day, and creating rituals that worked with her rebellious nature instead of against it.

By day 100, her Inner Jerk (aka Jory) had finally hushed for the first time in her life. She was getting more done than she had in years. Most importantly, she felt like herself again—and started dreaming of better tomorrows. So she wrote it all down.

Chandra has the super-sized value pack of undiagnosed learning disabilities, likely has ADHD and never thought she'd write a book like this—let alone a series. She created Wintering Well because feeling stuck and lonely, frankly sucks. If this helps just one person get unstuck and moving forward with intention, maybe they'll help someone else, and so on. The world needs more people living their lives on purpose, determined to make things better than they found them.

She lives in way-out west Austin, Texas with her family, can throw-down in the kitchen, and is finally working in her darkroom again after years of avoiding it. Her hope is that this workbook series will let her create enough artistic experiments that lead to a retrospective at the MoMA. Hey, a girl can dream.

www.ingramcontent.com/pod-product-compliance
Lightning Source LLC
Chambersburg PA
CBHW062109290426
44110CB00023B/2754